THRIVE!

Keys to Enjoying A Life of Purpose and Fulfilment

Volume 1

Yemi Akinsiwaju

© 2017

THRIVE!

Keys to Enjoying A Life of Purpose and Fulfilment

Volume 1

First published in Great Britain by Dayspring Publishing
Copyright © Yemi Akinsiwaju 2017
First published in paperback in 2017

The rights of Yemi Akinsiwaju to be identified as the author of the Work has been asserted by him in accordance with the Copyright, Designs and Patents Act 1988.

All rights reserved. This book is protected by the copyright laws of the United Kingdom. No part of this publication may be used, distributed or reproduced by any means, graphic, electronic or mechanical, including photocopying, recording, taping or by any information storage retrieval system without the prior written permission of the author except in the case of brief quotations embodied in critical articles or reviews.

ISBN (Paperback) – 978-0-9934482-3-2
ISBN (Hardcover) – 978-0-9934482-4-9

Unless otherwise noted, Scripture quotations are taken from the Holy Bible, New King James Version®. Copyright © 1982, 1984 by Thomas Nelson, Inc.

To order additional copies of this book, contact:
Dayspring Publishing Ltd
Tel: +44 (0) 208 469 3738
Email: orders@dayspringpublishing.com

Dedication

To my precious daughters, Oluwaseun, Toluwalope, Oluwatosin and Eniola… The true measure of success is living a life characterized by the discovery, pursuit and fulfilment of the divine purpose for which our Eternal Creator allowed you to step into this planet.

I dedicate this book to you and your generation of fellow leaders who will not settle for conforming to the shifting sands of popular societal norms and philosophies, no matter how alluring they may sound.

This book is dedicated to you as leaders with strength of character who embrace and live by the noble moral values anchored in the ancient truths of The Bible. These truths have withstood the test of time and continue to enrich the lives of those who seek true wisdom that honours The Creator and benefits humanity.

To you, my treasured daughters and to you my highly esteemed reader who seek the keys that enable the fulfilment of the great potential that resides within you, dare to soar as Eagles, release your greatness and leave a godly legacy that enriches your generation and beyond.

You Have Made A Difference. Thank You!

By purchasing this book, you have donated towards enhancing the life of someone in need.

Profits from this book will go towards charitable causes including the work of the following organisations:

Shalom Nagar Lepers Colony:

A place of refuge and life empowerment, run by New Wine International, for lepers and their families in Chennai, India.

Idanre Development Foundation:

Dedicated to fighting poverty, facilitating educational development and raising the quality of life for the underprivileged in Idanre town, Nigeria.

International Third World Leaders Association:

Actively involved in transforming followers into leaders and leaders into agents of positive change in over 80 developing countries.

ACKNOWLEDGEMENTS

I believe that there is no such thing as a self-made man or woman and all that we ever achieve is a product of the contributions of many other people into our lives.

This book epitomizes this principle… it is the product of many minds that have shared ideas and principles that have been of tremendous benefit to me in my life's journey thus far.

I am indebted particularly to the myriad authors who penned the books of the Bible as the creator of the universe inspired them.

To my lovely wife, Abi, thank you for your love, patience and partnership. To my precious daughters, Seun, Tolu, Tosin and Eniola, I love you very much and celebrate the unique treasures of wisdom and purpose that God has deposited in you for this generation and beyond.

To my Pastor, Michael Olawore, your life of courage, faith, servanthood, mentorship, vision and love for God and His people continues to inspire me… thank you!

My wonderful parents, Emmanuel and Grace Akinsiwaju… You served as my first and ongoing indelible introduction to the powerful expression of the many principles shared in this book… I am forever grateful to you and love you eternally.

Lanre, my brother… you are simply the best brother anyone could ever ask for… Thanks for being you.

Thrive!

To my mentor, Dr Myles Munroe, thank you for introducing me to the truth of The Kingdom of God and for challenging me to truly discover, pursue and fulfil my purpose... I am incredibly blessed by the privilege of having known you. Your legacy lives on through me!

To you, the reader, I commend your passionate pursuit of wisdom that will enable you to live more effectively and enrich humanity with the unique potential inside you. Thank you for choosing '**Thrive**' as one of the tools to assist you in your journey.

Finally and most importantly, to the source of ultimate truth and wisdom, God Almighty... THANK YOU!

CONTENTS

Dedication vii
Thank You ix
Acknowledgements xi
Foreword xv
Introduction 1
Insights 3
About the Author 129
References 131

Foreword

This book is a "reference manual"; a wealthy compendium of insights and key success principles that will empower you to thrive in life; a must-read for those who seek to live beyond average.

The insights contained in this book are revelatory, informative, directional and life transforming. Everyone should aspire to read through at least once a year; and refer to it as often as possible.

Yemi, I salute you for your passion and commitment to serve this generation and beyond; and for the priceless insights contained in this book. I am confident that significant value has been added to humanity as a result of this work.

You have truly encouraged this generation to live beyond the boundaries of limitations!

Michael Olawore
Snr. Pastor
New Wine Church Global Network

INTRODUCTION

Many people who profess to be Christians, unfortunately, view the Bible simply as a religious book for spiritual devotions and extract from it only the information that they feel would help them in their journey towards 'Heaven' (however, they may define this).

Many non-Christians, unfortunately, view the same book as a religious relic that no longer has any relevance to modern day society.

However, I have found, like many people through the ages, who are much wiser than me, that the Bible is a powerful collection of time-tested, battle-proven, life enhancing "God ideas" that when properly explored, understood and applied are able to equip anyone with an open mind, with the tools to change their lives dramatically. It offers the power to expand your capacity to achieve great contributions towards enriching our collective human experience.

The Bible expounds on many laws of success that govern virtually all the facets of life, where every human, regardless of your religious/spiritual persuasion, desires real and lasting victory. These include:

- Keys to harmonious human relationships

- Principles of personal and business success

- Precepts for healthy spiritual development

- Keys to effective leadership
- Many other ideas for living effectively and positively impacting other people's lives

This book is a compendium of ideas and distillation of key success principles gleaned from my learning from great leaders and from studying the Bible as a manual for effective living. I have been privileged to share the ideas with thousands of people over many years around the world either in person or in articles that have been credited with transforming the lives of many readers.

I offer this volume in the fervent hope that something you read in here will stimulate your thinking, energize your spirit, re-invigorate your creativity and act as a catalyst for the release and maximization of the tremendous potential within you so that you can thrive and fulfil your unique purpose for being.

I also hope that it will stimulate every reader, Christian and non-Christian alike, to revisit the Bible with a fresh attitude of inquiry and desire to truly experience the wisdom that lies within the pages of the most comprehensive manual for success ever penned.

I celebrate you and honour your passion for true wisdom and personal growth… Keep Soaring.

Yemi Akinsiwaju

(The Leadership Catalyst)

INSIGHTS

The Law of Dominion

Many people desire to accomplish something great with their lives. You may dream of impacting your generation with some noble idea, masterful invention or worthy virtue.

And all this is a legitimate expression of the spirit of dominion God has placed within you. When our creator said in Genesis 1:26, "*Let us make man in our image, after our likeness: and let them have dominion over the fish of the sea, and over the fowl of the air, and over the cattle, and over all the earth...*" He placed within you the ability to do what He had commanded.

... And that capacity for dominion is what seeks expression in the desire for greatness.

However, it is critical to understand that the pursuit of greatness is not simply the attainment of public acclamation. It is first and foremost the achievement of internal self-discipline motivated by the discovery of God's assignment for your life.

Achieving public glory without private victories over self is a recipe for disaster. Wise King Solomon stated this principle in the following words, "*He that does not rule over his own spirit is like a city that is broken down and without walls.*"[1]

A graphic demonstration can be found in the story of a former President of the United States of America. He ruled the political world but failed to rule his private passions. Consequently, his legacy to the world is tainted by scandal and moral deficiency. His name is now a byword for comedians in reference to sexual impropriety.

Greatness lies within you, my friend, but you must first exercise dominion over yourself before you exercise it in the public arena. And you must ensure that this remains the order of priority as your sphere of influence in the public arena grows… internal before external.

Our ultimate leader, Jesus the Christ exemplified this idea when he faced temptation in the privacy of the wilderness. Satan tried to coax him into public displays of power by jumping from the pinnacle of the temple at Jerusalem, but Jesus overcame this temptation (see Luke 4: 1 – 14). And because He ruled His passions and attained personal mastery, He achieved His ultimate goal of salvation for humanity and eternal dominion over the universe. So Remember… *Personal mastery precedes public glory!*

That is the law of effective dominion. Obey it, and the manifestation of your greatness is simply a matter of time.

Purpose and Effective Living

One of the keys to your effectiveness is the understanding of your purpose for being on earth. Your assignment on planet earth is so crucial that although God already had almost seven billion other humans, He caused you to be born. He endowed you with unique physical, mental, emotional and spiritual assets, tremendous capabilities and latent Omni-potency.

Your assignment on earth is so important that you need to discover it and live by it. Discovery of your purpose is the precursor of effective living. It is the basis upon which you can set the right priorities for your life.

Setting the right priorities serves diverse beneficial purposes in your life. These include:

- The protection and nurturing of those key relationships that bring real meaning to life and facilitate the achievement of the great dreams within you.

- The ability to protect the use of your time, and prevent you from abusing the time resource given you to fulfil your assignment

- The discernment of activities or people that will distract you from the pursuit of purpose.

Until you know what your destination is, all roads seem the same as they all lead to nowhere really important. However, once you get a sense of purpose (a clearly defined destination), you realise that travelling along just any road will simply not do. You now need a road map to get you to where you are going. Setting the right priorities serves as the road map that will help keep you on track towards destiny.

The most effective human to walk the face of the earth, Jesus the Christ, said to his followers many centuries ago "seek first the Kingdom of God and His righteousness and all these things (physical, financial and other resources) will be added to you ….."[2]

In essence, Jesus was saying to them, "Establish the right order of priorities." And as you live a well-prioritised life, underpinned by the pursuit of your purpose, all the resources you need for an effective life will begin to flow in.

This serves as a template for every human who seeks to achieve success even in the twenty-first century.

FAITH AND SUCCESS

The ancient writer of the biblical book titled Hebrews shares some profound truths about the quintessential attribute that makes for effective living – faith. He made the point that faith is a crucial prerequisite for those who desire to achieve great success, including having a dynamic relationship with our creator. Indeed, he proclaimed that without faith, it is impossible to please God!

But what is faith? Does the fact that you attend church every Sunday, read your bible studiously or sing the 'Christian' songs and speak the 'lingo' mean you have faith? Perhaps not… Faith, according to the greatest book ever written, "Is the evidence of things not seen and the substance (reality) of things hoped for."

This implies an aptitude to look into the unseen realms of the future and capture the purpose for your life in your consciousness, so strongly that they become your present day reality in your spirit and in your mind. And because they are now your reality, your daily actions are influenced to move you towards them.

The book of Hebrews is replete with examples of many olden day champions such as Noah, Abraham, Sarah and Moses who looked into their futures through the eyes of faith and accomplished great success and the purposes for their lives.

The one thing common to all these heroes of faith was this – they refused to conform to the limiting expectations of those around them or their mundane natural existence. Moses lived as a prince in Egypt; yet saw himself as the brother and deliverer of an enslaved people. Abraham and Sarah, although considered past childbearing age, looked beyond this natural limitation to see themselves as the father and mother of many nations.

Being a person of true faith may make you seem strange to those around you, and unfortunately, this is where many people go wrong. The desire to conform, so you don't stand out as 'strange' can become so strong that it begins to stifle the fulfilment of your destiny!

It is time to break out of this self-imposed limitation. The proof of your faith is that you are actively doing what you know in your spirit that you were born to do. You have a pervading sense of knowing that, "for this, I was born!" That purpose may not even lie within your current contexts, such as your current job, religious affiliation or business endeavour. Therefore, you have a responsibility to discover and pursue it.

The ultimate leader once asked this question of his followers, "When the Son of Man returns will He really find faith on the earth?"[3]

The answer to that question will be revealed in what you do today, tomorrow and henceforth in the pursuit of your purpose…

Champion With a Purpose

You made it into this year despite all that could have stopped you. Perhaps you had to overcome health challenges, emotional trauma, psychological distress and tremendous spiritual opposition aligned against you. *But You Made It!*

It is, therefore, my privilege to reach across the pages of this book, shake your hand and say, "welcome Champion, welcome to this year." Would you also kindly extend these greetings to any other champions around you and acknowledge that despite all that life threw at them in the last year, with the help of Almighty God, they came through.

Reach out and shake someone's hand, and tell him or her, *"Hello Champion, welcome to this year, your year of greater victories."*

And the source of those victories will be the Holy One of Israel, the **LORD GOD ALMIGHTY** who sustained you last year, even when it seemed He was far away. He is the one who has preserved you for His purpose and His plans. He reminds us today in the words of the prophet Jeremiah:

"For I know the thoughts that I think toward you, says the LORD, thoughts of peace, and not of evil, to give you an expected end.

Then shall you call upon me, and you shall go and pray unto me, and I will hearken unto you. And you shall seek me, and find me, when you shall search for me with all your heart."[4]

The LORD has preserved you because of the future He has in store for you. His thoughts have preserved you because of His eternal purpose for which He created you.

You had to overcome in the last year and enter this one because, *"you are his workmanship, created in Christ Jesus unto good works, which God had before ordained that you should walk in them."*[5]

The works God ordained for you await your complete mental focus, physical energy and spiritual faith this year. It will require you to seek after God in prayer with all of your heart and discover new dimensions of His presence than you ever experienced before.

You are a Champion for a purpose and with a purpose – Manifest it this year.

COMMITTED TO YOU

A wise leader in the early church had a profound insight into one of the keys required to be successful on the earth. He wrote, *"Behold what manner of Love the Father has bestowed on us, that we should be called the children of God...."*[6]

He had tremendous optimism based on his knowledge that we have access to an abiding, unyielding love that keeps you through every circumstance of life, even in the moments when you think all is lost and no one cares.

There is a popular poem called "Footprints in the sand" which graphically depicts this truth.

> One night I had a dream.
>
> I was walking along the beach with the LORD, and across the skies flashed scenes of my life. In each scene, I noticed two sets of footprints in the sand. One was mine, and one was the LORD's.
>
> When the last scene of my life appeared before me, I looked back at the footprints in the sand, and to my surprise, I noticed that many times along the path of my life there was only one set of footprints, and I noticed that it was at the lowest and saddest times in my life.
>
> I asked the Lord about it "LORD you said that once I decided to follow you, you would walk with me all the

way. But I notice that during the most troublesome times in my life there is only one set of footprints. I don't understand why you left my side when I needed you most."

The Lord said, "My precious child, I never left you during your time of trial. Where you see only one set of footprints, I was carrying you."

We are also reminded that *"neither death nor life, nor angels nor principalities nor powers, nor things present nor things to come, nor height, nor depth, nor any other created thing, shall be able to separate us from the love of God which is in Christ Jesus our Lord."*[7]

No matter who you are or what your past has been like, God loves you so much that even if you have fallen several times, He is willing to reach out to you one more time. He desires to hold you by the hand and pull you up from the dust of life's failures or defeats and place you right back on the path of destiny and righteous purpose.

He wants you to know today that *"I have loved you with an everlasting love and I have drawn you with my loving kindness."*[8]

God is committed to you and to your success!

FACING YOUR BATTLES

What do you do when faced with overwhelming odds and it seems that those who are against you are about to trample all over you? How do you respond when it appears that everything is stacked against you and you can see no way out?

Do what a wise king did!

Hezekiah, king of ancient Israel, faced such a situation when the most powerful army of his time, the army of Assyria came knocking at the gates of his city, Jerusalem. The Assyrians had such a fearsome reputation for their sheer brutality and destructive mentality that their presence was enough to send shivers of fear down the spine of those they confronted.

When Hezekiah faced the prospect of the destruction of his nation and himself, as recorded for us in the ancient texts,[9] he applied three key principles, which anyone serious about sustainable success can learn from and apply to his or her life.

a) **He confronted his fears in private** – Hezekiah did not fret and fuss in the presence of others, as many people tend to do when faced with troubles. He took his troubles to the temple and confronted them privately. Public fretting only serves to bring fear into the lives of others and reveals your lack of faith in the ability of God to rescue you.

b) **See your problem from a different perspective** – Hezekiah saw defeat in terms of it bringing an insult to the name of God and victory being a manifestation of divine power. He saw this simply as a battle in which God's name was at stake.

c) **Invite God into your situation through prayer** – This wise king acknowledged his dependence on God's supremacy and invited Him to fight the battle.

According to the text, God responded that He would defend Jerusalem for His own name's sake because He had a covenant with Israel and He keeps His covenant with those who love Him even unto their successive generations.

Friend, you have an everlasting covenant of love with God and whoever or whatever seeks your destruction pokes its finger at God's face.

Therefore, remember always, whenever you face difficulties, that you can and will emerge in victory as you apply the above principles.

VISION BEYOND YOUR TROUBLES

The capacity to see beyond the adverse circumstances of today to a brighter future you have envisioned is one of the core virtues that sets champions of life apart from everyone else.

It is important to note that everybody goes through pain at some point in life. People who choose to be victims collapse under the pressure of adversity, but the true champions of life see adversity as a temporary inconvenience and indeed as a stepping-stone to greatness.

One of the greatest heroes of the Christian faith, Paul puts it this way *"for our light, and temporary afflictions are working for us a far more exceeding and eternal weight of glory."*[10] This was said by a man who had gone through shipwreck, snakebite, painful beatings on several occasions, had been stoned and left for dead, experienced betrayal by friends, close pursuit by enemies, etc.

Yet he looked beyond these, refused to become a victim of his circumstances and emerged through his adversity to become eternally remembered as a champion of faith, responsible for penning more than half of the new testament of the Bible.

It has often been said, "When the dream is big enough, the facts don't count." Consider the ultimate leader *"who for the joy set before him, endured the cross, despising the shame thereof and sat down at the right hand of the throne of God."*[11]

Jesus, we are told, did not focus on the adversity of the cross; He saw it as a necessary part of the fulfilment of His purpose. Instead, He looked beyond it to focus on the majestic throne awaiting Him.

Dear friend, be encouraged to look beyond the adversities you face today; Rekindle the vision of glorious purpose and fulfilment that God has prepared for you and let it draw you onwards and upwards towards victory as you become the Champion you were born to be.

In Your Hands

One of the most recognised, yet neglected truth about human existence is found in the book penned by one of the wisest kings in human history. This truth is simply that, "A*s a man thinks in his heart, so he is.*"[12]

This implies that the responsibility for your present position and disposition in life cannot be ascribed to anyone else. The man in the mirror is fully accountable to God for the fulfilment of the gift of that life.

Your religious teacher, parents, teachers, the government, your boss, your ex-spouse, friends or any other candidate you may consider, cannot be held responsible for your life… Only you can!

The story is told of two young boys who caught a little bird and decided to test the wisdom of the wisest sage in their community. They determined that when they got to him, one would keep the bird behind his back as they asked… "Is the bird alive or dead?" If the sage said "alive", the bird would immediately be crushed behind the boy's back, and revealed to the sage as dead but if he said "dead," the boy would open his hands and let the bird fly away, thus disproving the wisdom of the sage.

The boys got to the sage and asked the question as planned. The wise old man smiled gently and responded, "Whether the bird lives or dies is up to you. Its life is in your hands."

And that response captures the essence of the responsibility that your Creator has placed upon you as a resident of this planet called earth. According to biblical truth, He has done everything He can to position you for tremendous success.

You were created to soar gloriously in the realms of fulfilled potential, to live a life filled with wonderful possibilities.

Let your mind be daily engaged in the pursuit of that purpose which our maker has uniquely deposited within you and as you do so, always remember that no one and nothing outside of you can stop the fulfilment of that destiny.

Why? Because God has placed the profound power and responsibility for failure or success squarely in your hands.

DWELLING IN THE SECRET PLACE

Events in the Middle East are once again rapidly gaining momentum and causing both economic and political instability around the world. Local news reports are daily filled with threats of employee strikes or political demonstrations, terrorist activity, health scares or economic crises of one form or the other. Most people are simply bogged down with a sense of despondency hoping that their personal lives will not be overtaken by the chaos seemingly all around them.

Yet this remains the finest hour for anyone who chooses to maintain a close relationship with the ultimate leader, Christ Jesus as the world around us cries out for an alternative to all the chaos they see and hear.

It presents the opportunity for effective leadership through a life that is filled with godly confidence, optimism and fearlessness.

What is the source of this confidence? Dwelling in the secret place of God!

We read in Psalm 91 that the benefits of dwelling in the secret place include:

- Deliverance from the traps set by your enemies
- Protection from diseases and epidemics
- Safety from unseen difficulties

- Confidence to triumph against satanic opposition
- Enjoyment of God's presence right in the midst of adversity
- Intimacy with God that brings automatic response when you call on Him
- Miraculous promotion in your endeavours
- Divine health and long life

Note however that the promises belong to those that dwell in the secret place and not to the transient, 'once in a blue moon' visitors. All of the blessings are available to those who will earnestly return to the secret place of prayer and the pursuit of godliness.

As you do so, the manifestations of a life lived in the secret place will mark you out like a light that is set on a hill that cannot be hidden. You will become a lighthouse of success and righteousness guiding the many ships of a hurting humanity around you into the harbour of God's love and peace.

The secret place awaits you…

The Quest for Significance

A wise man once said, "Don't settle for success; make a difference – Strive for significance."

True and long lasting significance is not often found in the arena of business accomplishments, financial or material acquisitions or the realms of artistic genius. Neither is it found in the exertions of religious activity.

Many people achieve so-called 'successes" in their careers, their business ventures or even their religious accomplishments but at the expense of meaningful relationships with other people.

True significance is found in the quality of our relationships. It is in the hearts of our friends, our children, our work colleagues, and our loved ones that the true measure of our stature is taken. Above all, it is in the quality of our relationship with God that life takes on real meaning and eternal significance.

The message of the Bible and the Kingdom of God is that of an eternal relationship; a Father's relationship with His children, first with Adam, the first man, then down through the ages with the people of Israel and now with you.

God's desire is for each one of us to come to know Him more intimately as Father, and He sent Jesus the Christ to reintroduce us to our heritage in Him. Furthermore, He desired that humankind develops the same depth and quality of relationships with one another that exists between Him and His first-begotten son.[13]

Dear friend, I invite you to take a moment to examine your relationships today. If every material thing you owned was taken from you today, how 'rich' would your life be? Jesus Christ gave up everything as He hung on the cross to atone for humanity's sins yet today, billions love Him passionately, and many are willing to give their lives for Him in return.

The world is crying out for genuine love where we truly give of ourselves to enrich the lives of others.

Reach out to all the people you meet today, and in the coming week, in genuine love and fellowship, because long after you are gone, you will be remembered, not for your material accomplishments but for the love you shared.

That is the gateway to significance!

OBEDIENCE: PATHWAY TO FULFILMENT

Obedience is one of the primary gateways into sustained success and great blessings. The scriptures are full of many injunctions to obey God's commands so that we may partake of all the goodness He has in store for us.

Sometimes people blame God, the devil, other people or even bad luck for the adverse circumstances they face. However, oftentimes the truth is that they are simply victims of their own disobedience. There are physical and metaphysical/spiritual laws that govern our existence on this planet, and if you wantonly break those laws, you will reap the consequences.

Obedience comprises two main components.

a) The first is knowledge. The Bible is quite clear about the perils of lacking knowledge and clearly shows that ignorance can be quite deadly. As is often said, if you contravene a traffic regulation and the police stop you, "Ignorance of the law is not a valid excuse for breaking it."

    It is therefore astonishing that many people do not invest sufficient time in studying and understanding the creator's requirements for effective living on His planet.

    God wants the very best for you, but in order to enjoy them, it is critically important to invest quality time in studying His principles and precepts and learning from others who have received profound insights into how this planet works. He wants the abundant fruit of righteousness, wisdom and favour to be manifest in your life but you have a part to play in receiving His goodness.

Investing the time to acquire relevant information will prepare you to achieve your tremendous potential in enriching humanity. There is no shortcut.

b) The second component of obedience is choice. Having knowledge is a critical foundation but correctly exercising your God-given privilege of choice and doing the right thing will mark you out for blessing and greatness in the Kingdom of God.

My fervent hope is that as you pursue the keys to wisdom and success, seek to be the best that you can be and achieve all that you are capable of achieving; you will also diligently focus on obedience to your loving creator and thereby enter into the fullness of purposeful living.

The Value of Prayer

Prayer is the act of communion with our heavenly Father. It is the backbone of an effective life. Most Christians and people of other religious faiths will agree that prayer is very important (even if they feel uncomfortable with calling it prayer) but unfortunately, it is one of the least understood and least developed facets of many people's lives.

At the heart of effective prayer is love for God and love for His creation. A genuine love for God always motivates us to spend time in His presence.

Simplicity, Secrecy and Sincerity are the three watchwords that characterise effective prayer. The most effective human to have walked the planet earth, Jesus the Christ, taught His followers about prayer with the following words:

"And when you pray, you shall not be like the hypocrites. For they love to pray standing in the synagogues and on the corners of the streets, that they may be seen by men. Assuredly, I say to you, they have their reward. But you, when you pray, go into your room, and when you have shut your door, pray to your Father who is in the secret place; and your Father who sees in secret will reward you openly. And when you pray, do not use vain repetitions as the heathen do. For they think that they will be heard for their many words."[14]

The quality of your prayer life is a reflection of your love for God. However, He loves you to be yourself. If you are highly intellectual and the high-sounding vocabulary is a true reflection of yourself, by all means, use it in your communion with Him, always remembering that He sees your heart. If simple words or no word at all is a reflection of whom you are, God understands that too.

The principle, in essence, is 'Be Yourself!' That is simplicity, and God loves it.

If the vast majority of your prayer life is confined to what happens in the public arena at religious prayer meetings, sorry, that is self-deception. Your creator wants time with you privately. There are things He will only talk to you about in private. That is one of the hallmarks of a love relationship. God values the secret place… you should too.

Above all, your heart is what matters. Until you enter into His presence in sincerity and with love for Him and for the humans he has created in His image, rather than with a selfish agenda to get Him to do 'your thing', prayer is simply an exercise in futility.

Dear friend, your quest for a successful life will be supercharged when you understand the value of prayer and apply its unimaginable power to your life.

WHERE ARE YOU?

One of the most potent questions ever asked is the question "where are you?"

According to the biblical records, this was the question God asked of our prime ancestor, Adam in the Garden of Eden after he had succumbed to the temptation to make the wrong choice.

That question remains as powerful today as when you and I were still locked in the genes of Adam, the very first man on planet earth and God asked him this question.

At the beginning of creation, God had given Adam a dominion mandate, a directive, within certain beneficial restrictions, to rule, manage, cultivate and govern all the resources of the earth and thereby manifest the glory, wisdom and power resident in him. The mandate Adam received also defined the Omni-potential and ability to fulfil it.

However, Adam flouted the restrictions, and this wrong choice led him to disobey God's command and thereby terminate the ability to maximise his potential. So when God asked Adam, 'Where are you?' Adam was forced to confront the truth about himself.

It is a question that will force you also to confront some crucial truths about your life. These include:

- Who you really are – You are created in the Image of God and to fulfil His glorious purpose. Does your self-image align with this truth?

- Who or What you have become – Are you living below your true potential and why?

- Where you are heading – Ask yourself, "If I keep doing what I'm doing, will I achieve the true success that enriches my life and others' and fulfil my purpose for being?"

- The consequences of your choices – What changes and new choices must I make?

As you approach the end of this day, it is crucial to explore your answers to God's question, "Where are you?" It is time to take stock, to evaluate your choices and your results in the light of all that God has promised you and the potential that He has placed within you. As an ancient philosopher once said, 'a life unexamined is a life not worth living.'

As you encounter the truth in your answers, may the truth you unveil release you into divine freedom to become all that you were born to be in the rest of this year and beyond.

GET BACK UP AGAIN

There is a promise in the scriptures to everyone who chooses to do right as you strive to fulfil your assignment and the purpose for which you were born. The promise is this, *"Though the righteous fall seven times, the LORD will raise him up again."*[15]

Okay, you've made mistakes, you've taken some wrong turns, and you've fallen flat on your face..... Several times too.

But Arise! A man does not drown by falling in water; you drown by staying there. Arise from the dust of defeat, from wallowing in self-pity, from the mire of condemnation and the negative opinions of other people.

It's a new day, an opportunity to start afresh, to resume the pursuit of purpose, to shake off the shackles of the past and step into a future filled with promise.

God is not finished with you yet; you are a work-in-progress. We are reminded that *"many are the afflictions of the righteous, but the LORD delivers him from them all."*[16]

Perhaps you feel like Christ did as he hung on the cross, alone, ashamed, abandoned and mocked by onlookers. Yet within you whispers that inner voice which says, "So must it be, that the Kingdom of God may be established on the earth through you."

Just as a sculptor hammers and chisels out a magnificent sculpture out of wood or stone, your afflictions and failures are not meant to destroy you, they are the tools that chisel out the flaws and weaknesses of your character and reveal the image of greatness within you.

Allow God to shape your character as He teaches you the valuable precepts and principles of His Kingdom to be learned from your experiences. Don't get bitter; Get better!

Great biblical figures such as Paul, Peter and Moses had moments of failure, but they overcame these to become legends of faith. God qualifies you for greatness through the development of your character, and your character is shaped by how you respond to failure.

So stretch forth your hand and place it in the Lord's hand. Let Him pull you back onto your feet. Get back up again and march forward…Onwards and Upwards into the fulfilment of your God-ordained purpose.

Run Your Race

"Do you not know that those who run in a race all run, but one receives the prize? Run in such a way that you may obtain it."[17]

This admonition from Paul the apostle, one of the most effective leaders in human history is worth considering if you desire to live a successful life.

There are many people who show up at work, at their religious institutions, in their homes or in any other arena of life and that is pretty much all they really do; they simply show up. However, the message from this great leader is loud and clear… Just showing up is not enough. Simply being in the race is not enough!

Your entry into the race must be for one purpose… To win the prize!

This reinforces the idea that your life should be lived with a sense of godly purpose, a pursuit of divine destiny and a desire to win.

One of the most frequent remarks of successful gold medallists in the Olympics is simply, "I ran my race." This remark highlights the principle of mental and physical focus. While there were other contenders for the gold medal who were running hard right beside them, they didn't focus on what the others were doing. They focussed totally on their own strategy for winning. They ran their own race and won.

God has an assignment for you; a race He has designed with you in mind; that race is uniquely yours, and no one else can run the race quite like you; you were wired to win that race. The strategy for winning that race will come from Him. Spend time with God in the place of prayer to obtain that strategy.

In addition, it will take all of your physical, mental and spiritual focus and discipline to carry out that strategy. Paul put it this way, "everyone who competes for the prize is temperate in all things" and "I discipline my body and bring it into subjection."[18]

God designed you to win, He desires for you to win, and He enables you to win by the power of His Holy Spirit given to you; but only you can run the race. Do not try to run someone else's race… that is the recipe for failure.

I trust that as you choose to run your race, you will be able to say in the fullness of time, just as Paul did:

"I have fought a good fight, I have finished my race, I have kept the faith; Henceforth there is laid up for me a crown of righteousness, which the Lord, the righteous judge, shall give me at that day: and not to me only, but unto all them also that love his appearing"[19]

The prize awaits you!

WALKING BY FAITH

A glorious future awaits you as you pursue the purpose for which you were placed on this planet. There are dimensions of that future that have already manifested themselves in your present and in which you are walking.

However, other aspects of that future are still unknown to you and remain a mystery of God's destiny for your life.

For those mysteries of the human experience, many people approach them with a sense of fear or trepidation. Others approach them with a defeatist attitude; one, which assumes that life, is out to 'get them'. There is, however, a third approach which the Bible recommends. This is the attitude of faith.

As someone who is committed to living victoriously through the time-tested principles and precepts outlined in the scriptures, we are enjoined to *"walk by faith, not by sight."*[20]

This implies you should not live your life based simply on the limitations of your physical senses but live in a realm that transcends those senses.

The Bible defines faith as "the assurance of things hoped for, the evidence of things not seen" and makes the point that heroes of biblical history earned their place in the hall of fame through their determination to walk by faith.

Walking by faith is not some spiritual mumbo-jumbo that some Christians use when trying to sound impressive. Rather, it is an attitude of the mind that demands courage in the pursuit of a God-given objective. It is founded on one simple premise… A clear understanding of what God has said to you!

All the heroes of faith outlined in the biblical book of Hebrews had one thing common to them – they had received a specific instruction or promise from the Creator, and that word served as the anchor upon which they were willing to live and if necessary, die. Which is why the Bible tells us that, *"faith comes by hearing the word of God."*[21]

So what specific instruction or promise from God is serving as your anchor? What objective has He set before you that you are actively pursuing and demands every ounce of courage within you?

Until you have clear answers to these questions, it is doubtful whether you are truly walking by faith. However, if you are actively pursuing the divine purpose for your life based on the principles of love for God and for humanity created in His image, you are headed in the right direction.

If your pursuit is also based on the firmest conviction of the nobility of your assignment and its value towards enriching the human experience, then you are truly walking by faith, and God is well pleased.

THE LAW OF REPRODUCTION

Every seed reproduces after its own kind! That is the law of reproduction ordained by the creator of the universe since the dawn of creation, which affects many dimensions of human existence. He instituted this law by the following words, *"Let the earth bring forth grass, the herb yielding seed, and the fruit tree yielding fruit after his kind, whose seed is in itself, upon the earth"*, and it was so...[22]

An understanding of this law of reproduction is crucial in the pursuit of an effective life.

Many people desire great things for their lives. They go to bed each night wishing for a better life filled with wonderful blessings. Yet their lives are filled with quiet desperation and unspoken frustrations because they ignore the fundamental laws that have been set in place to guarantee their success.

One such law is that your harvest today comes from the seeds you sowed yesterday. Therefore, to reap the desired harvest, you must sow the correct seeds. Apples grow from apple seeds and oranges from orange seeds. You do not expect to reproduce oranges from apple seeds.

In the same way, you cannot sow the seeds of mediocrity yesterday and expect to reap a harvest of excellence today. Whatever harvest you desire for tomorrow, begin to sow the seeds today. Three important seeds to consider when sowing are:

The seed of God's word – Find passages in the Bible that pertain to your desired harvest (e.g. spiritual maturity, physical health, financial prosperity, etc.); meditate on them consistently until they take root in your heart.

The seed of discipline – Dr Mike Murdock is renowned for this profound quote, 'the secret of your future is hidden in your daily routine'. On a daily basis, weed out any ideas or activities contrary to the seeds of God's word you have sown. Furthermore, cultivate new daily habits and actions that are consistent with the seeds sown in your heart. This will allow the fruit of the word to come forth in your life.

The seed of positive confession – Speak into existence the godly harvest you desire. God has placed creative ability on your tongue[23], and you will eat the fruit of your lips, so make sure that your lips plant only positive seeds into your future.

As you consistently plant and nurture these seeds of truth, may they yield the fruit of God's abundant blessings in your life.

LESSONS FROM THE MOTHER

Mothers' day, which is celebrated in many nations is a day set aside to celebrate the unique contributions of mothers to our lives. It also provides the opportunity to explore some principles relating to motherhood that we can all apply to enhance our abilities to live lives that are more effective. These include the following:

All great things begin with a seed – The Bible admonishes us never to despise the days of small beginnings. Indeed the Kingdom of God is likened to a seed [24] and began with the seed promised by God at the dawn of creation.[25] That seed, Jesus Christ who was planted in Israel over two thousand years ago, has since blossomed into over 2 billion lives and is still growing.

Within you lies the seed of purpose. It may be revealed to you like a dream just like Joseph, the prime minister of ancient Egypt, or as an idea that simply would not let you go, much as it held Moses, the deliverer of Israel captive[26]. However it manifests, the simple truth is that the seed of greatness resides in you.

The seed comes from the father – simple biology teaches us that the seed does not come from the mother. She receives the seed from the father and incubates it in readiness for the appointed time. The seed carries the genetic characteristics of the father.

Similarly, the seed of destiny planted in you comes from your heavenly Father. His purpose for you carries His traits of greatness, righteousness and love for humanity. Whatever the dream you are pursuing, ensure that it does carry these traits otherwise you are pursuing the wrong dreams.

Nurture the Seed – Just like an expectant mother is advised to take the right foods and drinks and abstain from anything prejudicial to the well-being of the baby, your mission is to nurture the seed God has planted in you. Eat the right spiritual, intellectual and physical foods to preserve the well-being of the seed of God's purpose. Avoid thoughts, actions and people that are toxic to your future.

Expect and accommodate Change – Pregnancy brings physical, hormonal and emotional changes to the expectant mother. Wisdom dictates that the expectant mother anticipates these changes e.g. buy a new set of clothes to accommodate the increase in physical size.

It is remarkable that many people expect to achieve great success in their lives without a willingness to change. The simple fact is, if you expect to deliver greatness, you must prepare for and willingly embrace change.

Labour Pains – Always precede the arrival of the baby. No shortcuts! Prepare for the labour pains and if you are already going through them… Congratulations, you are about to bring forth your wonderful gift to humanity… Your purpose!

Now the Journey Begins – That of nurturing your divine assignment, which you have brought forth, into full maturity to impact the world with the glory of God.

SEASONS OF CHANGE

One of the fundamental principles of success is the law of timing. Discerning the times and seasons of life is crucial if you desire to accomplish the fullest purpose of God for your life. Solomon, the wise king, understood this principle when he wrote, *"To everything there is a season and a time to every purpose under the heaven."*[27]

Jesus Christ, the ultimate leader, once rebuked the spiritual leaders of Israel for failing to properly discern the season of life in which they were living.[28]

Throughout the scriptures, the catalyst for the transition has always been an instruction from God, faithfully acted upon at the right time by the recipient of the instruction.

Gideon received and acted upon the specific instruction he received from God, and this enabled him to make the transition from captivity to freedom.[29]

His obedience to God also marked a season of change for all the nation of Israel.

The disciples received and obeyed an instruction from God, which released Paul into one of the most prolific and world-changing apostolic ministries in history.[30]

The Bible draws attention to the men of the tribe of Issachar,[31] who assisted David in ascending the throne of Israel through their wisdom because they had an understanding of their times and knew what Israel needed to do to achieve victory.

In these days of global economic and political turbulence, your transition into your next season of victory will be closely tied to you hearing God's voice and obeying His instructions. It is therefore critically important to sharpen your discernment so that you can recognise your season of change, and like the sons of Issachar, respond appropriately to God's leading.

How do you do this? The same way the early disciples did it!

We must each return to the place of prayer and fasting, which sensitises us to the voice of God. There is a strong river of divine purpose and grace flowing throughout the world in these days. This river is bringing us into a season of change.

If you desire to partake of the glorious victories this season offers, now is the time to hear God's voice and return to the place of intimacy with Him.

Assured of His Presence

A decision to grow into spiritual maturity and walk in increasing measure of faith is a decision to step into the unknown. To become all that God has called you to be demands that you walk in dimensions you have never walked in before. Often, these steps of faith into greater dimensions are tentative and tinged with a sense of anxiety or insecurity.

At such times, it is wonderful to be reminded of God's promises that strengthen us in our mind and spirit. Over 360 times in the Bible, in one form or the other, God promises us *"fear not, for I am with you."*[32]

Whatever the next phase or season of life you enter, do so with this assurance of His presence. Let His promise never to leave you or forsake you[33] permeate your spirit and banish every sense of fear or trepidation.

God's abiding presence guarantees you the following benefits:

- Victory in warfare as God fights your battles – Israel repeatedly enjoyed this benefit as they cultivated God's presence through obedience to His word.[34]

- Guidance by His Spirit – Travelling in the uncharted territory of your future is made easier when the One who knows all things and holds the eternal GPS (Global Positioning System) is on your side giving you directions on how to get from where you are to where you need to go.[35]

- Abundant blessings on your life and your household – Obed-Edom enjoyed the privilege of having the Ark of the Covenant in his home for three months, and he became so blessed that even King David couldn't help but notice. Allowing the Holy Spirit have His free course in your life will position you for blessings beyond your imagination.[36]

God provides so many more benefits to those who will allow Him to have free reign in their lives and enjoy His unceasing presence.

In a world filled with so much change and uncertainty, the assurance of God's presence is a sure foundation upon which you can build a most effective and productive life that impacts this generation with your noble contributions.

LISTEN AND WIN

As the disciples witnessed the transfiguration of Jesus Christ on the holy mountain, the King of the universe leaned over the balustrades of heaven and declared, "This is my beloved Son, with whom I am well pleased, listen to him."[37]

We can learn the following very important principles from this experience of the disciples on the mount of transfiguration:

a) There are some things that God will show you only in private. You should, therefore, be willing to step away from the hustle and bustle of life to spend time alone with the Master if you want to experience His glory. Jesus separated Peter, James and John from the other disciples to spend time with Him privately so they could experience His Majesty.

b) When you enter His presence, listen to God's voice. Too often many people talk so much in the place of prayer and worship and never quieten down in their spirit long enough to discern God's Voice. The instruction from God to the first disciples at that mountaintop event extends to us today... "Listen to Him."

Now more than ever before it is critical to be able to hear God's voice. The world needs solutions to the myriad problems of religious conflict, economic instability, political confusion, educational chaos and health crises among others. Political and other types of community leaders are wallowing in confusion and struggling to come up with ideas to resolve the problems.

In essence, a lot of the traditional ideas and approaches to problem resolution are proving insufficient to meet the needs of the twenty-first century; which is why we need to tap into a wisdom that is beyond this world.

Only the wisdom of God is able to resolve most of these problems, and you obtain this by listening to His voice in the private place of prayer.

c) Obey your instructions - Jesus instructed His disciples not to reveal His glory to the world until the appropriate time. Similarly, there is an appropriate time for you to reveal and apply the great ideas revealed to you in private. The important thing is to discern the correct timing and then take appropriate action.

As you experience the glory of God's presence, hear his voice and obey, get ready for the greatest outpouring of blessings and good success in your life.

THE SUN OF RIGHTEOUSNESS

In temperate climates, as summertime approaches and the sun shines brightly each day, you'll likely observe that more people are smiling and have a pleasant disposition towards life. There is something about the warmth and brightness of the sun that positively impacts the human experience.

Nature also responds to the sun just as brightly... flowers blossom, beautiful butterflies flit around and busy bees are energised as they buzz around pollinating the flowers and making sweet honey.

But all of these are nothing, compared to the inner glow and warmth that impacts every dimension of your life when you allow the eternal sun of righteousness into your heart.

The Bible records, *"Unto you that fear my name shall the Sun of righteousness arise with healing in his wings; and you shall go forth, and grow up as calves of the stall. And you shall tread down the wicked, for they shall be ashes under the soles of your feet in the day that I shall do this, says the LORD of hosts."*[38]

This sun is Christ Jesus, who lights up the life of every person who truly accepts Him, with a radiance that dispels gloom and brings healing that restores you physically, emotionally and spiritually

Christ's presence also brings the following benefits according to the passage above:

Progress – **You shall go forth** – because God sets you free from the burdens of past negative experiences and the shackles of present low expectations, you are released to become all that God has designed you to be.

Maturity – **And grow up** – You receive greater wisdom and understanding to handle life more competently.

Fruitfulness – **As calves of the stall** – Where there was once barrenness, you become fruitful, producing bountiful, life-enriching essence (like the calves' fresh milk), which nourishes others.

Victory – **And you shall tread down the wicked** – With God on your side, your physical and spiritual enemies become as nothing (like burnt ashes)

There is a dimension of purposeful, victorious, abundant living that is possible only when you allow Jesus Christ to have full rein in your life.

And when you do so, the sun of righteousness shines radiantly through you, bringing warmth, hope and love into the lives of others within your sphere of influence.

YOUR DECISIONS...YOUR LIFE

"There are many plans in a man's heart; nevertheless the counsel of the LORD, that shall stand."[39]

This comment from the wise king, Solomon highlights the need for each one of us to seek the mind of our creator and understand His will for our lives before we make important decisions and plans.

What you have and what you are today is, to a very large extent, the accumulated product of the decisions you made in your many yesterdays. Your decisions are a product of the quality of your thinking… and your thinking is a product of your knowledge.

Therefore, if your knowledge is flawed or deficient in some major respect, the quality of your decisions will be very poor, and consequently, your actions will yield poor results.

This simple principle explains why life is a joyless exercise in frustration for many people. This is why it is also crucial to yield to the admonition that *"Wisdom is the principal thing; therefore get wisdom: and with all your getting, get understanding."*[40]

And pure, life-enhancing knowledge and wisdom comes from God who desires the very best for you. There are three key benefits of seeking divine insight as part of your decision-making process:

- **Reduction in frustration and wasted effort** – since God's purpose will prevail anyway, it makes sense to align yourself with Him so that you don't waste your time and efforts pursuing objectives that will displease Him and are therefore unattainable.

- **Guarantees answered prayer** – James, a leader in the early church stated, "*You ask, and receive not, because you ask amiss, that you may consume it upon your lusts.*"[41] If you desire the joys of answered prayer, the prime directive is "seek the will of God" and then pursue it.

- **Assures peace and victory** – When you understand the will of God and align your decisions with it, His peace floods your heart, and He releases divine power to enable you to accomplish that which pleases Him. As a result, your success is assured.

As you seek first the Kingdom (the mind and purposes) of God; all those things which are beneficial to you and which will facilitate your quest for sustainable success will be given to you.

NO GOOD THING WILL HE WITHHOLD

Many people believe a lie that has been sold to many millions of people around the world down through the ages. For some reason, they have accepted that God does not want them to have the best things in life. They accept poverty and mediocrity as their lot in life and settle for a sorry existence.

Yet this idea runs contrary to even a cursory look at the scriptures. Many passages such as those below paint a completely different picture for us.

"Let them shout for joy, and be glad, that favour my righteous cause: yes, let them say continually, let the LORD be magnified, which has pleasure in the prosperity of his servant."[42]

"For the LORD God is a sun and shield: the LORD will give grace and glory: no good thing will he withhold from them that walk uprightly."[43]

The word upright conjures the image of someone who is steadfast, forthright and unwavering in the pursuit of righteousness and all that God has promised them.

David was anointed as king of Israel as a youth but had to remain steadfast in his belief that what God had promised He would bring to pass. It took about twenty years, but God did not withhold the good things He had promised. David simply had to grow into it.

That principle applies to you as well; God delights in your prosperity, but you must be willing to grow into it in righteousness, knowledge and wisdom.

You must never again accept the lie that average is enough. God wants the BEST for you. He does not want to withhold any good thing from you.

Stretch your thinking, develop your God-given talents and abilities and make your heavenly Father proud of you as you fulfil the fullness of the righteous purpose for which He caused you to be born.

SEASON OF UNYIELDING PRAYER

Whenever you enter a new season of private or corporate destiny, there is always an increased demand on you to respond appropriately to God's prompting to "come up higher."

The transition into your new season of accomplishment must also become a transition into a season of unyielding prayer. This is crucial because as a discerning man once stated: "every new level forces you to encounter new challenges."

God has promised you some blessings, but you must be willing to take hold of them in persistent, unyielding prayer until you see their physical manifestation.

A biblical account demonstrating this principle is recorded for us in the following passage:

And Elijah said unto Ahab, "Go up, eat and drink; for there is a sound of abundance of rain." So Ahab went up to eat and to drink. And Elijah went up to the top of Carmel; and he bowed himself down on the earth, and put his face between his knees, and said to his servant, "Go up now, and look toward the sea." And he went up, and looked, and said, 'there is nothing."

And he said, "Go again" seven times. And it came to pass at the seventh time, that he said, Behold, there arises a little cloud out of the sea, like a man's hand. And he said, "Go up, say unto Ahab, Prepare your chariot, and go down, lest the rain stop you." And it came to pass in the meanwhile, that the heaven was black with clouds and wind, and there was a great rain."[44]

Just as Elijah experienced, the transition from drought and barrenness into fruitfulness, revitalisation and abundance requires persistence in prayer.

You simply must be willing to go the extra mile until you obtain results. Elijah did not stop praying when the feedback he received remained negative. He held a firm conviction that change was imminent and he maintained his commitment to effective, fervent prayer until the physical manifestation of his faith showed up.

Like the famous prime minister of Great Britain, Sir Winston Churchill once proclaimed, "Never, Never, Never, Never, Never give up."

This admonition is especially relevant to anyone who has chosen to go beyond the ordinary into the realms of extraordinary achievement. It will take a never-say-die attitude in prayer and positive, faith-reinforcing action to see your dreams of success manifested.

Your victory awaits you on the other side of the river of persistent prayer.

PASSING THE TEST

Many Christian believers are convinced that we are living in 'the last days' that the Bible foretold over two thousand years ago. To support this assertion, there is a keen focus on continually interpreting political events and natural disasters as a fulfilment of biblical prophecy.

While some of these events may indeed be a fulfilment of those prophecies, many of them often do not directly impact us and our best response is through prayer and support for those who have been directly and adversely affected.

There is, however, one aspect of 'the last days' for which you will be held directly accountable and responsible because the power to affect the outcomes lies within you.

That aspect relates to the attitudes that we cultivate and live by and is found in the following words of the apostle Paul to his protégé, Timothy:

"But know this, that in the last days hard times will come, for men will be lovers of themselves, lovers of money, boastful, arrogant, blasphemers, disobedient to parents, ungrateful, unholy, without natural affection, irreconcilable, malicious slanderers, without self-control, brutal, haters of good, betrayers, reckless, conceited, lovers of pleasure rather than lovers of God"[45]

Jesus the Christ, the ultimate leader also referred to a critical deficiency that would characterize these days in the following words *"And because iniquity shall abound, the love of many shall wax cold."*[46]

Many people around the world are still wallowing in strife and refuse to be genuinely reconciled with those who have hurt them in the past while some others love pleasure more than spending time with God in prayer, worship or obedience to His word. Indeed, one of the most potent criticisms of religion (whatever form it takes) is its contribution to violence, hatred and destruction of human potential in many nations of the world.

So, what about you? Your prime responsibility as an honourable citizen of this planet, who is committed to true success that honours our Creator and blesses mankind is to continually undertake a robust self-evaluation test in relation to the characteristics listed above by Paul… Do any of those words describe your behaviour or attitude? If yes, it is time to make the necessary corrections.

Above all, the one test you must pass is that of your love for God and fellow humans. Is it growing cold? If yes, Please rekindle it urgently because Jesus promised that only a person that endures (in love) unto the end, will experience true salvation.[47]

Only true love for those you serve will make your contributions to your family, community or nation live long in the hearts of men.

THE HEART OF A CHILD

According to the scriptures, Jesus Christ came to earth to reinstate the Kingdom of God, established at the very beginning of time, which Adam had lost through disobedience in the Garden of Eden.

Jesus stated, *"When the Son of man shall come in his glory, and all the holy angels with him, then shall he sit upon the throne of his glory; And before him shall be gathered all nations: and he shall separate them one from another, as a shepherd divides his sheep from the goats. And he shall set the sheep on his right hand, but the goats on the left. Then shall the King say unto them on his right hand, "Come, you blessed of my Father, inherit the kingdom prepared for you from the foundation of the world."*[48]

One remarkable thing is that although the Kingdom, with all its benefits and promises is available to you, it is still possible to miss out on it or those benefits if you lack one fundamental requirement… the heart of a child.

Jesus explained, *"Allow the little children to come unto me, and forbid them not: for of such is the Kingdom of God. Verily I say unto you, whosoever shall not receive the Kingdom of God as a little child, he shall not enter therein."*[49]

The 'heart of a child' encompasses some crucial success attitudes or mindsets such as:

Innocence – a little child is pure in motive. When they act, it is without malice and even where there are disagreements, they easily forgive and return to unconditional love.

Persistence – children, do not easily take 'no' for an answer. This attitude of persistence positions them to receive blessings because they simply will not give up.

Curiosity – Their enquiring mind enables them to access a vast range of information as they try to make sense of their world. In the same way, you must remain open-minded as the Holy Spirit leads you into deeper truths and opens up the secrets of the Kingdom to you. A mind closed by spiritual or religious dogma is deprived of experiencing some of the most profound experiences that God would love to share with you.

Pure faith – A child simply believes! If you promise something, they will continually remind you until you fulfil it, because they believe. God desires the same attitude of faith from all His children, you and me.

Fail their way to Success – How does a child learn to walk, write, or talk? He or she simply fails his or her way to success. Children are not afraid of failure. They will keep falling down and getting up until they learn to walk competently. That must become your attitude too.

I encourage you today to cultivate the heart of a child and step into the fullness of the greatness prepared for you.

Heavenly Testimonial

'And when God had removed Saul, he raised up unto them David to be their king; to whom also he gave testimony, and said, "I have found David the son of Jesse, a man after mine own heart, which shall fulfil all my will."' [50]

What a powerful testament to the character and the pursuit of righteousness. What would God say if we had a chance to obtain a testimonial about you?

Unfortunately, many religious people or those who profess spirituality, including many Christians cannot be said to be after God's heart. They're after His gifts, power or blessings… but not His heart. They're more interested in what they can get out of Him and not particularly interested in developing an intimate relationship with Him.

However, if you asked them a direct question about this, they would protest vehemently that you dared to question their spirituality or love for God and wax lyrical about how much they loved and had a relationship with the creator. But just saying it doesn't make it necessarily so….

How do you know when someone is really in love? By how much time they are willing to spend in the presence of the one whom they love and their willingness to change to accommodate the desires of that person. That same principle holds true in your relationship with God. The proof of your love is in how much time you do spend with Him. And the more time you spend with Him, the clearer you understand

His heart, know His will and change your ways in order to please Him.

We have this further testimony about David:

"Nevertheless for David's sake did the LORD his God give him a lamp in Jerusalem, to set up his son after him, and to establish Jerusalem: Because David did that which was right in the eyes of the LORD, and turned not aside from anything that he commanded him all the days of his life, save only in the matter of Uriah the Hittite."[51]

However, without knowing His heart and will, how can you truly obey Him? So in essence, intimacy leads to obedience. And obedience delights God's heart.

David's intimacy with His heavenly Father and commitment to living by the success principles outlined in the ancient scriptures equipped him to become one of the greatest kings in Jewish history.

It is my prayer that your genuine love for the true and living God will grow stronger each day and draw you closer to Him in the secret place of prayer and worship and as you do so, may the heavenly testimony be "I have found………….(your name) a man / woman after my heart"

FOCUS ON THE DREAM

What do you do when life seems to take strange turns and twists, and events appear to be conspiring against your success or even your very existence? How do you respond when those people whom you trusted desert you and those who remain, do not believe in your dream or your ability to fulfil the mandate of God upon your life?

Do what the ultimate leader did!

'Jesus the author and finisher of our faith; who for the joy that was set before him endured the cross, despising the shame, and is set down at the right hand of the throne of God. For consider him that endured such contradiction of sinners against himself, lest ye be wearied and faint in your minds.' [52]

Jesus Christ did not focus on the imminent pain of the cross, nor did He focus on the betrayal of His friends or the actions of His persecutors. Instead, He focused on the dream!

Christ, our ultimate example of success, focused on the joy of sitting on the throne beside the Father, and everything He went through paled into insignificance in comparison with this goal.

Do you have a dream powerful enough to live for and if necessary, die for?

Jesus did... and that is why He reigns today as the author and finisher of our faith.

Without such a God-inspired dream, life becomes overwhelming because your difficulties become your total focus and this drains you physically, mentally, emotionally and spiritually. The molehill does indeed become a mountain.

However, when you develop the kind of destiny-focused goals that Jesus did, you become more than a conqueror because even when you walk through the valley of the shadow of death, you will fear no evil because God is with you.

Terrorism, religious extremism, financial crises and any negative life event no longer has any power over you, because He who began that great dream in you is faithful to complete it.

When things seem so difficult that it seems you are barely hanging on by your fingernails, it is time to ignore the nail clippers and let those nails keep growing fast so you can keep hanging on.

At such times, your mission as a champion of life is to focus on the dream and the giver of the dream.

WHAT DO YOU SEE?

One of the fundamental distinguishing characteristics of the greatest contributors to human history is their ability to see the invisible and believe in the impossible.

This ability called 'Vision' is the critical essential, which separates the truly great from the mediocre. As a wise man once said, "Eyes that look are common but eyes that see are truly rare and uncommon." So the question arises "What do you see?"

Do you only see the situations and circumstances around you? Or do you only see the opportunities to buy your house, buy your car, grow your bank account and take your holidays? Or are you able to look into the invisible and capture a vision of your destiny, which transcends you and leaves a legacy for future generations?

The Bible proclaims an eternal truth, which if you ignore it, will, unfortunately, number you amongst those most mediocre of humanity who goes to the grave with the treasure of God's best, still buried in them.

That truth is simply this: "*Where there is no vision, the people cast of restraint, lack discipline and ultimately perish.*"[53]

Abraham, the father of Israel, caught a vision of his destiny as the father of many nations as God brought him outside, and said, "*look now toward heaven, and tell the stars, if you are able* to number them: and He said unto him, so shall your seed be." And he believed in the LORD; and he counted it to him for righteousness.'"[54]

Joseph also captured the vision of His purpose, which eventually brought him to leadership in Egypt (see Genesis 37: 3 – 41: 4).

Capturing the vision of God's purpose for your life is one of your greatest weapons against the possibilities of a wasted life.

- *Vision protects you from pursuing the good at the expense of the best.*
- *It enables you to carefully select the persons whose company you keep*
- *It gives you a sense of confidence and holy boldness that sets you above average*
- *It gives you an assurance of victory in the face of overwhelming obstacles*
- *Vision creates a dynamic pull, which draws you upwards in the pursuit of destiny*

If you will live a life of fulfilment and touch yours and future generations for good, seek the face of the author of your destiny and capture His vision for your life. Only then, will you have the God-inspired answer to the question… what do you see?

PURIFIED

Many Christians sing a certain song joyfully, especially when they are feeling 'spiritual'. The song goes:

Purify my heart; let me be as gold and precious silver

Purify my heart; let me be as gold, pure gold

Refiner's fire; my heart's one desire; is to be holy…

And what such soul-stirring words these are.

However, what happens when God answers this 'cry of your heart'? How does gold become pure? Or how does silver become precious?

By being put through fire!

God spoke about this process through Zechariah the prophet:

"And I will bring the third part through the fire, and will refine them as silver is refined, and will try them as gold is tried: they shall call on my name, and I will hear them: I will say, It is my people: and they shall say, The LORD is my God."[55]

The Bible describes you as the workmanship of God, created in Christ Jesus to do the good works prepared for you before the world began.[56] So, although the works had already been prepared, now you have to be prepared for those works.

A skilled craftsman does not refine wood or straw by using fire; he knows the fire will destroy it. Only the right type of material is refined by fire.

The fact that your heavenly Father, the ultimate craftsman allows you to go through the fire of testing means only one thing… *You are the right material, and He sees you as gold or silver!*

An understanding of this principle is so important to enable you to maintain the right attitude in the midst of your refining process.

The apostle James understood this when he wrote, *"My brethren, count it all joy when you fall into diverse trials; knowing this, that the trying of your faith works patience. But let patience have her perfect work, that you may be perfect and entire, wanting nothing."*[57]

So when next you sing that wonderful song, remember what it means…You are saying, "I am precious in God's sight like gold" and I am willing to go through the furnace of purification that will purge me of all things that contaminate the excellence, power and glory of God resident within me.

So let it be…

The Way of the Master

"Let this mind be in you, which was also in Christ Jesus: Who, being in the form of God, thought it not robbery to be equal with God. But made himself of no reputation, and took upon him the form of a servant, and was made in the likeness of men. And being found in fashion as a man, he humbled himself and became obedient unto death, even the death of the cross.

Wherefore God also has highly exalted him and given him a name, which is above every name. That at the name of Jesus every knee should bow, of things in heaven, and things in earth, and things under the earth; And that every tongue should confess that Jesus Christ is Lord, to the glory of God the Father." [58]

The above passage reveals God's pattern for true success in the life of anyone who truly wants to be a world changer in his or her arena of influence.

a) The first step is self-discovery and mental reconditioning – Jesus the Christ knew He was God and His choice to take on human form did not in any way reduce His sense of whom He was.

You are also created in the image and likeness of God (see Genesis 1: 26) and your current station in life must never be allowed to reduce your sense of self-worth or self-esteem.

b) Secondly, Jesus the Christ voluntarily chose the humility of obedience to God the Father and service to humankind.

The Christ chose to be a servant. Similarly, if you intend and expect to achieve the greatest and best that God has ordained for you, obedience to God, in service to humanity, is the divine pathway.

c) Finally, God exalted Jesus the Christ to His right hand and placed Him over and above everything, or being, in creation. And this is a thought that escapes too many people – Your Creator and Father desires to exalt you and place you in leadership within your organisation, your local community and your nation... Yes, You!

God wants sons who have the same mind as the Christ[59] to rule and reign on the earth, but you must learn to follow in His footsteps and apply His pattern:

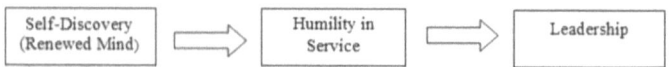

This is the way of the Master.

BEHOLDING HIS GLORY

The Bible is the undisputed best-selling book of all time, not only because of its claims, as the word of the Creator of the universe, is the most validated text (as confirmed by archaeology, molecular science, quantum physics, etc.), but also because it contains the most profound, time-tested principles. Wise men through the ages have used these principles to transform their lives from mediocre existence to purposeful, generation-impacting living.

Some of these principles are revealed in the following extract from a record of an encounter that the Jewish prophet, Isaiah had with the God of Israel:

> *"In the year that king Uzziah died I also saw the Lord sitting upon a throne, high and lifted up, and his train filled the temple. Above it stood the seraphim: each one had six wings with two he covered his face, and with two, he covered his feet, and with two, he did fly. And one cried unto another, and said, Holy, holy, holy, is the LORD of hosts: the whole earth is full of his glory. And the posts of the door moved at the voice of him that cried, and the house was filled with smoke.*
>
> *Then said I, Woe is me! For I am undone; because I am a man of unclean lips, and I dwell in the midst of a people of unclean lips: for mine eyes have seen the King, the LORD of hosts. Then flew one of the seraphim unto me, having a live coal in his hand, which he had taken with the tongs from off the altar: And he laid it upon my mouth, and said, Lo, this has touched your lips;*

> *and your iniquity is taken away, and your sin purged.*
>
> *Also, I heard the voice of the Lord, saying, "Whom shall I send, and who will go for us?" Then said I, Here am I; send me. And he said, Go, and tell this people, "Keep on hearing, but do not understand; and keep on seeing, but do not perceive."*[60]

This experience produced the following results in Isaiah's life:

a) **Forced an honest self-evaluation** – Isaiah encountered a higher standard of righteousness in God that forced him to conclude that his talking patterns (and therefore his thinking habits) required a major upgrade. Similarly, until you undertake a true and honest assessment of whom you really are, effective living is impossible, because you continually operate out of self-deception.

b) **Transformation** – Isaiah was transformed from a sin-filled person with unclean lips, and evident low self-esteem, to a righteous, courageous powerhouse who influenced his nation with godly counsel and is still influencing the world over two thousand years later through his writings.

c) **Discovery of his assignment** – Isaiah was introduced to his assignment and his real purpose for being when he met God. In the same way, if you desire to live victoriously instead of living a frustrated life as a wandering generality, the discovery of who you are and why you were created is found only in the mind of your creator.

Discover the Kingdom

A fresh look at the life and teachings of Jesus, the Christ reveals a truth that has remained hidden from many Christians and non-Christians over the centuries. This simple truth is that *Jesus did not bring a religion called Christianity*. In fact, the Bible tells us that it was pagans in Antioch who first labelled the believers in Jesus as Christians.[61]

What Jesus brought to mankind was the restoration of the Kingdom of God on earth. The Kingdom of God refers to the dominion and influence of God working through humans on the planet earth. That is what the first man, Adam, lost through disobedience to God and that is what Jesus, the Christ (also called the last Adam)[62] came to restore.

When He taught His disciples to pray, He taught that our prayer should take the form of *"Your Kingdom come, Your will be done on earth as it is in Heaven."*[63]

The bible also states clearly, that *"And Jesus went about all the cities and villages, teaching in their synagogues, and preaching the gospel of the Kingdom…"* and when Jesus sent His disciples out to preach, He also commanded them what to preach in the following words *"And as ye go, preach, saying, "the Kingdom of heaven has arrived"*[64]

Many Christians see their religion (other religions do the same) as an escape pod to heaven but Jesus Christ, in contrast, prayed that God would not take those who believed in Him out of the earth (see John 17: 15 & 20) but leave them here to fulfil His Kingdom mandate. The ultimate prize He promised

His followers are revealed in His words "...*Then shall the King say unto them on his right hand, Come, ye blessed of my Father, inherit the Kingdom prepared for you from the foundation of the world...*"[65]

And as a warning to those impressed by their participation in church activities and demonstrations of spiritual power, Jesus proclaimed "*Not everyone that says unto me, Lord, Lord, shall enter into the Kingdom of heaven; but he that does the will of my Father which is in heaven.*

Many will say to me in that day, Lord, Lord, have we not prophesied in your name and in your name have cast out devils? And in your name done many wonderful works? And then will I profess unto them, I never knew you: depart from me, you that work iniquity."[66]

So the responsibility of every person reading this today is to return to the scriptures to understand the message of the Kingdom, discover the will (predetermined purpose and pleasure) of God for your life (which might be to influence business, politics, education, music, film industry etc.) and then live effectively to fulfil that purpose.

HOLD FAST

In a season when everything that can be shaken is being shaken, is there an anchor upon which you can place your trust and which cannot fail you? The answer is a resounding YES!

And that anchor is faith in a promise made by God to you. This is not a reference to some mistaken concept that some Christians practice in which they simply lift any scripture out of the bible and quote it as a personal promise. Such a practice only results in endless frustrations, as God is not obligated to sanction stupidity.

However, you can place your faith in God's word. It is a faith that must rest upon a sure Word from the Almighty, which absolutely resonates with your spirit not just with your intellect. It is a Word that brings calm to your spirit in the midst of utter chaos. It is a revelation of God's purpose for you for that season that brings you through every difficulty.

God obligates Himself to honour a faith that rests upon such a sure word, as he orchestrates the universe to fulfil His purpose. He proclaims through the prophet…

"Remember the former things of old: for I am God, and there is none else; I am God, and there is none like me, Declaring the end from the beginning, and from ancient times the things that are not yet done, saying, My counsel shall stand, and I will do all my pleasure: Calling a ravenous bird from the east, the man that executes my counsel from a far country: yes, I have

spoken it, I will also bring it to pass; I have purposed it, I will also do it"[67]

"For as the rain comes down, and the snow from heaven, and returns not there, but waters the earth, and makes it bring forth and bud, that it may give seed to the sower and bread to the eater: So shall my word be that goes forth out of my mouth: it shall not return unto me void, but it shall accomplish that which I please, and it shall prosper in the thing whereto I sent it. For you shall go out with joy, and be led forth with peace: the mountains and the hills shall break forth before you into singing, and all the trees of the field shall clap their hands."[68]

Remember His promises to you or return to His presence in prayer and fasting so you can hear the voice of God.

And as you receive His promises... *Hold Fast*... Remain tenacious in your convictions that you will accomplish victory despite any opposing circumstances. It shall be accomplished just as God promised you.

THE PRIVILEGE OF ANOTHER DAY

Congratulations… you've made it into another day. And this means God is not finished with you yet. The assignment for which you were created is not yet completed, and you have one more day in which to fulfil your purpose on earth to the glory of God.

As David, a wise king understood, *"Your eyes did see my unformed substance, in your book all my members were written, every one of them,* **the days that were ordained for me, when as yet there was none of them***. How precious also are your thoughts unto me, O God! How great is the sum of them."*[69]

Whatever the mistakes or successes, pains or pleasures of yesterday, the fact that you are alive today is conclusive proof that there is more to be accomplished. There is more that God expects of you, to advance His Kingdom on earth and enrich mankind.

The Bible tells us that *"we are his workmanship, created in Christ Jesus unto good works,* **which God has prepared beforehand that we should walk in them.***"*[70]

A brief look at the landscape of present day human experience leaves us in no doubt that mankind needs help. We are in short supply of good works that is required to bring radical transformation to a world filled with strife, disease, injustice, moral perversion and many other things that debase humanity.

Hence, our planet needs the God-inspired good works that you can contribute to making our world a better place.

Whose life will be better today because your life touched theirs?

How will the world be a better place because you lived today?

The responsibility to make today count is yours and yours alone. How will you invest it?

If you have not yet received Christ Jesus into your life, today is your day. Now is your chance to enter into the Kingdom of God and reset your life on course to becoming all that a good God has in mind for you. Note that we are not talking about a religious experience that simply bombards you with irrational dogma and fear of eternal loss when you do not measure up to some warped ideology of God.

We are talking about reconnecting with a loving heavenly Father, through a heartfelt decision to repent i.e. change your mindset from one of rebellion and opposition to God to one that embraces His love and grace towards humanity. Then living each day with a deep desire to know and live by God's life-enhancing principles.

If you are already a citizen of His Kingdom, what will you do today in the pursuit of that purpose which God prepared in advance for you to fulfil?

You have the privilege of another day… Invest this gift wisely.

ARE YOU LISTENING?

As the world responded to the impact of one of the worst natural disasters to hit North America with the possible loss of over 2000 lives, one was left pondering how such an appalling loss of life could occur in the most technologically developed nation on planet earth today.

With all the advanced weather warning systems and human and financial resources available to them, the United States of America was caught flat-footed by Hurricane Katrina.

While our hearts went out in prayer and goodwill to all the people affected, it is important to remember how Jesus, the Christ responded to a similar scenario, which happened over two thousand years ago and which is recorded for us in the following words...

And Jesus answering said unto them, "do you suppose that these Galileans were sinners above all the Galileans because they suffered such things? I tell you, No: but, except you repent, you shall all likewise perish. Or those eighteen, upon whom the tower in Siloam fell, and slew them, do you think that they were sinners above all men that dwelt in Jerusalem? I tell you, No: but, except you repent, you shall all likewise perish"[71]

In essence, these kinds of events are a trumpet call to genuine repentance. Not the kind of repentance that entails emotional trips to the altar of many churches or other religious institutions, accompanied by insincere tears; But a genuine change in attitude and conduct which proves conclusively that you have had an encounter with the truth that has set you free from your past mindset of rebellion towards God.

God wants a people distinguished by righteousness, love and godly faith to demonstrate His true nature to a hurting world. He wants the world to see His children, born of His Holy Spirit, manifesting His glory to all of the creation.

God wants to develop a people committed to excellence, passionate about enriching humanity whom God loves, dedicated to living victoriously in all dimensions of their lives and above all, people who are a genuine signpost of unadulterated love and kindness.

The Bible reminds us again that… *"God who at sundry times and in divers manners spoke in time past unto the fathers by the prophets, has in these last days spoken unto us by His Son, whom he has appointed heir of all things, by whom also he made the worlds…"*[72]

The LORD is speaking clearly to everyone who seeks true and lasting success but are you listening?

Knowing Him

The present age that we are living in demands emotional and spiritual strength that is beyond the ordinary. It is an age marked by tremendous religious conflict, political turbulence, civil disobedience, health epidemics, natural disasters and previously unimaginable spiritual tension and hunger for truth.

This hunger for truth and craving for spiritual satisfaction is so great that many millions around the world have become easy targets for purveyors of false religions who promise them 'inner peace' but are unable to deliver on this promise.

In essence, the words of the prophet Daniel, penned over 2,500 years ago are being fulfilled right before our eyes. He wrote, "***And such as do wickedly against the covenant shall he corrupt by flatteries****: but the people that do know their God shall be strong, and do exploits.*"[73]

Against this backdrop of spiritual hunger is the urgent need for people who know their God, the only true and living God of Israel and Father of Jesus, the Christ to arise with a renewed sense of purpose and a passion for the lost.

It is time for YOU to arise and do exploits (wonders, accomplishments) in this generation, which demonstrate the spirit of excellence and anointing for success your heavenly Father has deposited within you. Your exploits may be in the arena of politics, business, education, entertainment or other areas of human endeavour.

But doing exploits is underpinned by a deep, abiding knowledge of the Creator and His established principles for success. And knowing God comes with a price that is quietly outlined by the ultimate leader in the following words, "***If you love Me, you will keep My commandments***. *And I will ask the Father, and He will give you another Helper, that He may be with you forever; The Spirit of truth, Whom the world does not have the power to receive because it neither beholds Him nor knows Him.* ***But you know Him because He abides with you and will be in you.***"[74]

The price of knowing God is obedience and intimacy.

Obedience - demands personal knowledge of the biblical truth (please note that I did not say religious dogma or long held denominational doctrine, but Bible truth!). Biblical truths have passed the tests of longevity, historical accuracy, scientific enquiry and transformational human experience. It is guaranteed to bring you sustainable success.

Intimacy - demands a passionate commitment to a lifestyle of persistent prayer, love for the presence of God and love for mankind.

Knowing Him is our key to success in the present dispensation, and the price is non-negotiable.

THE MARK OF RIGHTEOUSNESS

Many centuries ago, Paul, one of the leading lights of the early church, received insight from God into what the days just before the return of Christ would be like.

He expressed this revelation to his young protégé, Timothy in the following words…

"But know this, that in the last days hard times will come. For men will be lovers of themselves, lovers of money, boastful, arrogant, blasphemers, disobedient to parents, ungrateful, unholy, without natural affection, irreconcilable, malicious slanderers, without self-control, brutal, haters of good, betrayers, reckless, conceited, lovers of pleasure rather than lovers of God; Holding to a form of godliness, although they have denied its power; turn away from such men as these"[75]

His insight reads like a running commentary on the state of our nations and the prevailing attitudes of the hearts of people today.

Notice that one of the hallmarks of the age was 'having a form of godliness, but denying the power thereof'. This refers to the religious hypocrisy that is so common amongst many 'church folk' today.

This hypocrisy is manifested through a predisposition towards engaging in religious activities for its own sake. They regularly attend church services, sing the right songs, say the 'hallelujahs' and the 'bless you' but live a life that is devoid of the power of the Holy Spirit.

God does not want you to be numbered amongst a people whose life is filled simply with religious performance. He wants you to be branded with His mark of righteousness. He wants your life to be an expression of His Kingdom on earth. He wants you to be a walking, talking dynamo of excellence and success in the arena of life in which you operate.

In the physical environment, the greater the darkness, the more the glory of light is revealed. This is paralleled in the spiritual environment too. As the world seems to grow darker through the evil of terrorism, prejudice of all sorts, moral laxity and intellectual corruption where people claim falsehood as the truth, the light and glory of the Almighty God is meant to shine brighter through you, because you are the light of the world.[76]

The LORD desires that you be a spiritual dynamo that impacts wherever you are, but this will only come through your living in the understanding that *"the Kingdom of God is not eating and drinking, but righteousness and peace and joy in the Holy Spirit."*[77]

As you walk in the righteousness and power of the Holy Spirit, His mark of righteousness will set you apart for success and glory in this age and in the age to come.

Change Your Focus

When life seems to throw you a sucker punch and catch you off balance and defeat seems to be staring you in the face, it is a natural human response to feel despondent and descend into the cosy arms of self-pity.

But… that is not the response of a champion!

At such times, you must learn to look beyond yourself, the circumstances, the taunts of your enemy and the inabilities of your friends to offer real comfort. At such times, you must correct your focus and learn to look to the God of eternity.

You must look to the One who has demonstrated His unfailing love for you throughout the years, even during the times when you did not know Him.

And when you correct your focus, you enter into the dimension of heartfelt praise which David, the beloved king of Israel experienced when he penned the following words:

"Praise ye the LORD. Praise the LORD, O my soul. While I live will I praise the LORD: I will sing praises unto my God while I have any being. Put not your trust in princes, nor in the son of man, in whom there is no help. His breath goes forth, he returns to his earth; in that very day, his thoughts perish. Happy is he that has the God of Jacob for his help, whose hope is in the LORD his God:

Who made heaven, and earth, the sea, and all that therein is; who keeps truth forever.

Who executes judgment for the oppressed; who gives food to the hungry. The LORD looses the prisoners. The LORD opens the eyes of the blind. The LORD raises them that are bowed down. The LORD loves the righteous. The LORD preserves the strangers; He relieves the fatherless and widow, but the way of the wicked he turns upside down.

The LORD shall reign forever, even your God, O Zion, unto all generations. Praise ye the LORD."[78]

As your heart soars in the knowledge of Christ's love for you, remember these promises:

"You shall bring them in, and plant them in the mountain of your inheritance, in the place, O LORD, which You have made for You to dwell in. In the Sanctuary, O Lord, which your hands have established; The LORD shall reign forever and ever."[79]

When you decide to change your focus from your challenges to praise, you interrupt the stream of despair and become infused with a new sense of optimism for a better future. Renewed optimism energizes your creativity and inspires innovative solutions to whatever challenge you are facing.

Always remember, what you focus on magnifies, so choose carefully what you focus on.

The Creative Word

There are situations that arise in life that seem to defy a solution. You have stepped out 'in faith' in pursuit of a dream, vision, calling, goal, however you describe it, in response to what you were absolutely convinced was God's will.

And then things come to a grinding halt. You experience a setback that feels like an insurmountable obstacle. At such times it is tempting to think that God has deserted you or that He is unsympathetic to your cries for help and you wish that you had never set out in pursuit of that goal.

Regardless of what some misguided friends, implacable opponents, anyone else or even your own inner voice of doubt may proclaim, nothing could be further from the truth.

Many millennia ago, Israel, a people chosen by God, acting upon His instructions came out of slavery and entered a wilderness in pursuit of His vision and promise to them... Then things seemed to go awry.

They experienced such hunger that they complained about their leaders, Moses and Aaron and wished that they had never been delivered from slavery. However, God had a different perspective on their experience, revealed in the following words:

"And he humbled you, and allowed you to hunger, and fed you with manna, which you did not know, neither did your fathers know; that he might make

you know that man does not live by bread only, but by every word that proceeds out of the mouth of the LORD does man live."[80]

This shows that God sometimes allows and uses 'difficult' experiences to equip His children and bring them to higher realms in three key areas.

a) Humility – God allowed the experience so that Israel would recognize the subtle lure of pride which had ensnared their hearts, and return to God in humility.

b) Knowledge – The experience exposed them to a new level of knowledge of God's truth that they were previously oblivious to. They now knew about supernatural provision even beyond what their fathers could teach them. In much the same way, crisis exposes you to a new dimension of creativity and ingenuity that normal times often do not.

c) Effective Living – The new knowledge arising from this experience taught them to place greater value on the words of the God who had supernaturally delivered them from captivity. For you as well, the principles and ideas that emanate from God and that are recorded in the Bible have the creative capacity to raise you to a new dimension of effective living.

So, when you face trials… rejoice! And remember God's perspective. You are simply being prepared for a greater dimension of effectiveness. The word of The LORD never fails, and He will bring you into your promise.

REFLECTIONS

As the year progresses, it is appropriate to regularly reflect on how your year is going; to take stock of where you are, where you have been and where you are going. It is a time when you engage in honest, personal evaluation of your life and performance in the context of one key question…

"Have I fulfilled the plans and purposes of God for my life this year?"

The Bible records a parable of three servants given talents of gold by their master, which underlines the principle of performance evaluation.[81]

Each one of them received an assignment and resources to fulfil their assignments, and their master went on a long journey, leaving them to fulfil His assigned purpose. *"After a long time, the lord of those servants returned, and settled accounts with them."*[82]

The time of reckoning revealed that two of them had accomplished their master's purpose, but the third one had not only failed to fulfil his master's purpose but also began to give excuses in order to absolve himself of responsibility for his failure.

What if the third servant had taken time out to honestly evaluate his performance before his master returned? Wouldn't that have given him a chance to correct his underperformance and obtain better results before the ultimate day of reckoning?

Dear friend, the master has placed tremendous resources and opportunity in your life; how far have you utilised them in advancing the Kingdom of God this year?

Remember, however, that it is not a matter of what you have done compared to others but "What have you done compared to what you ought to have done?"

Your answers should lead you to the next set of questions namely:

- What does God want of my life this year? – Spend time with Him in prayer to discover His purpose for you.

- How does He want me to accomplish His purpose? – Devise the plans by the leading of His Holy Spirit.

- How do I know when it is done? – Include measurable objectives that will enable you to evaluate your performance.

As you cultivate the practice of godly reflection and honest, purpose-driven self-evaluation, may you ultimately hear the master say the words, *"Well done, good and faithful servant; you were faithful with a few things, I will put you in charge of many things, enter into the joy of your Lord."*[83]

Keep your Heart Pure

Jesus the Christ, the ultimate King, in His famous 'sermon on the mount,' outlined the essential personal qualities and character traits that will position you for great success.

One of the qualities He articulated is purity of heart. He expressed this requirement in the following words, *"Blessed are the pure in heart for they shall **see** God."*[84]

The word translated as 'see' is the Greek word 'optonomai' that implies being transfixed in awe by a scene of absolute, breathtaking wonder. In essence, Christ was teaching us that in order to experience the glorious, manifest presence of our heavenly Father, the Lord of all creation, it would take more than singing a few songs in church, saying a few hallelujahs or following an unchanging routine of religious activity.

It would require having a pure heart in the sight of Him who knows all that you did last night, all that you have said this morning and all that you are thinking right now.

Despite what you may have heard to the contrary, God has indeed handed to you the responsibility for maintaining a pure heart, while providing the instructions for meeting His requirement.

Three absolute essentials for keeping your heart pure are found in the following instructions.

a) *"Therefore if you bring your gift to the altar, and there remember that your brother has something against you; Leave your gift at the altar, and go your way; first, be reconciled to your brother, and then come and offer your gift."*[85] This means God takes your relationships with other people more seriously than your efforts to please Him with religious activities or attendance at church.

b) *"...And all of you, clothe yourselves with humility toward one another, for "God opposes the proud, but gives grace to the humble."*[86] Great kings and kingdoms have been brought down because of pride. If you will experience God's presence, avoid pride like the plague.

c) *"Guard your heart with all diligence; for out of it are the issues of life."*[87] Just as you protect your physical home against unlawful entry, you have to protect your heart against ungodly entry. Wrong ideas (those which keep you from seeking God's presence and pursuing your God-ordained purpose) from television, radio, books, friends, the internet and other sources of information are always seeking unlawful entry into your mind. Erect strong barriers against them.

May you experience supernatural victories and the glory of God's presence more than ever before as you purify your heart before Him in the days to come.

The Pursuit of Righteousness

According to Jesus Christ, the most effective leader to ever influence this planet, the number one priority for every human and the fundamental key to success is to "*Seek first the Kingdom of God and His righteousness....*"[88]

In order to avail ourselves of this success key, it is important to understand what Jesus meant by the words, 'His Kingdom' and 'His righteousness.'

The Kingdom of God on earth is the fulfilment of God's eternal purpose and sovereign rule in the earth. As someone dedicated to maximizing your potential, your mandate is, therefore, to discern God's purpose and yield your life as an agency through which that purpose is accomplished.

And this leads us to the principle of righteousness. Too many religious people are caught in the trap of confusing 'religious' activities tied to their particular persuasion with true righteousness. However, righteousness simply put, is 'doing the right thing'... And doing the right thing is closely interwoven with purpose.

Suppose you invited me to your house this morning as a car mechanic to fix a defective car that you intended to take on a crucially important trip later this afternoon. You leave me with your car keys and leave home for a while, fully expecting to return and find your car fixed.

What if I looked around and saw your garden was in need of attention and then I entered your garden, weeded it, planted some beautiful flowers, and landscaped it immaculately… But I did not fix your car. It is most likely that you would return home and be very, very upset with me.

Why? Is it because the garden wasn't lovely? No, it is because that is not the purpose or the reason for which you invited me to your home. I had done a good thing but not the right thing, and because I failed to do the right thing, your planned trip to undertake a very important project was now in jeopardy.

That scenario describes the lives of too many people. God has created you, designed you and brought you into His Kingdom to fulfil a specific assignment but many people are busy being busy. They are doing good 'religious or charitable' deeds but not fulfilling the divine assignment God has purposed for their lives… And God is not impressed!

So if you desire to walk in righteousness this year, I appeal to you to return to God, the author of your life, with a humble and seeking heart and discover His purpose for your life. Then pursue that purpose with every fibre of your being.

In essence, the pursuit of righteousness is the pursuit of 'the right thing', your God-ordained purpose.

WHAT IS IN YOUR HAND?

Perhaps you have come to the realisation or caught glimpses of the truth that you have been born to accomplish a specific assignment and divine purpose in this generation.

Then the questions arise in your heart…"How will I accomplish this task that God has entrusted to me?" Do I have the necessary tools, skills, or credibility to embark on this important life-project?

If those questions have arisen in your heart, congratulations! Welcome to the club of World Changers. One of the founding members of this elite World Changers Club, also listed in the Faith Hall of Fame (see Hebrews 11), received a direct commission from God and had to deal with similar questions.

This man, Moses, had an encounter with God that interrupted his life of mediocrity and set him on a new purpose driven pathway.

However, in order to make this transition, Moses had to face and conquer his self-imposed limitations and the fear of other people's opinions. This is recorded in the following passage:

"And Moses answered and said, but, behold, they will not believe me, nor hearken to my voice: for they will say, The LORD has not appeared to you. And the LORD said to him, what is that in your hand? And he said, "A rod."

And God said, Cast it on the ground. And he cast it on the ground, and it became a serpent; and Moses fled from before it. And the LORD said to Moses, Put forth your hand, and take it by the tail. And he put forth his hand, and caught it, and it became a rod in his hand."[89]

Moses already had in his hand, the instrument to fulfil his assignment but he saw it as a mere shepherd's staff or rod. In the same way, God has already placed in your life what you need to get started in fulfilling His purpose. However, you have to see them from His divine perspective, not yours.

Pursue the presence of God until you receive His insight on how that which He has placed in your life will serve His purpose.

When you receive this life-transforming insight, you are liberated from the fear of self-inadequacy or the fear of people. You become a world changer like Moses who *"took his wife and his sons and set them upon an ass, and he returned to the land of Egypt: and Moses took the rod of God in his hand."*[90]

Like Moses, you no longer see your gifts and abilities as a mere shepherd's rod but as the rod of God in your hand with which you will achieve great things.

TRUE WISDOM

The Late 20th and early 21st Century have come to be known as the information age primarily because of the proliferation of knowledge around the world.

At the click of a mouse, you can obtain information on almost any subject on the Internet.

Indeed, it is estimated that the service industry (which is predominantly the movement of information) makes up almost 60 percent of the multi-billion pound British economy.

However, knowledge is not wisdom....

Many educated fools abound in our nations. They have acquired so much knowledge that they have become a clear manifestation of the Psalmist's words:

"The fool has said in his heart, there is no God."[91]

And that is why your nation needs you. We need a new generation of leaders like the young Jewish man, Daniel, in the ancient kingdom of Babylon, who will not only be exceptionally knowledgeable in their fields of endeavour (see Daniel 1: 4 & 17) but will also have that critical extra called wisdom.

The psalmist identified wisdom thus:

"The fear of the LORD is the beginning of wisdom: a good understanding have all they that do his commandments: his praise endures forever."[92]

You see, knowledge without moral restraint is the foundation for the destruction of an individual, a nation or even a civilisation.

This is why the clarion call is going out to you… Like Daniel, seek to excel in the areas of life where God has placed you. Don't let the loud voices of the mediocre drown out the quiet, yet powerful ideas of the excellent.

Then add to your knowledge, wisdom. Walk in the fear of the Lord and obey His Commandments. Let His word be the moral compass that continuously guides your life and makes you an example worthy of following.

Such a life is the essence of true wisdom.

Transformed by His Word

Global communications through television, radio and the Internet, exposes us each day to a deluge of bad news. Mudslides in the Philippines, Islamic sectarian violence in Iraq, religious conflict in Nigeria, murders and crime of all sorts in the United Kingdom, Iranian and Palestinian threats to destroy Israel continually stream out of the news media and fill people, many believers included, with a sense of fear.

The niggling questions at the back of most minds include, "what is happening to our world? How will this affect me? Is the world coming to an end soon?"

However, be at peace dear Child of God, you have been born for such a time as this… The glory of the light is revealed by the depths of the darkness in which it shines.

Jesus the Christ had already prepared us for these times when He said, *"these things I have spoken unto you, that in me you might have peace. In the world you shall have tribulation: but be of good cheer; I have overcome the world."* [93]

As the world seems to grow darker, the light of Christ in you must shine ever brighter. Every environment you enter must experience the glory of God's Kingdom, which is righteousness, peace and joy in the Holy Spirit. [94]

This means they can now experience righteousness where ungodliness once prevailed, peace where confusion, hopelessness and fear once held sway and joy where despair and sorrow once reigned.

To become this effective agent of change, you must be willing to overcome your personal fears and limitations and be transformed into your inner being by God's Word.

Peter the Apostle had this breakthrough experience (see Matthew 14: 25 – 33) as he walked on water in obedience to one word from Jesus, "Come!"

For as long as Peter's heart and mind were filled with that word from Jesus, he overcame the natural laws of matter and experienced the supernatural. Similarly, you can be transformed by one word from the LORD today.

Fill your mind with the powerful truths in the Bible and allow God to quicken them in your heart.

When this happens, you will step out into the realms of faith that reveal the glory of God and His mighty power at work in you… You will transform your world.

FRIENDS WITH THE KING

The most powerful gift any leader can give you is the gift of access. Access to the presence of a king is the gateway to intimacy, favour, influence and tremendous blessings.

Consider this… If Her Majesty, Queen Elizabeth of the United Kingdom invited you to her palace to have lunch with her several times and then made it known publicly that you had access to her 'as a friend', what do you think would happen to your standing in your local community or even throughout the United Kingdom?

You would become a celebrity overnight!

The Media across the country and perhaps even around the world would be falling over themselves to meet you and get some insight into your relationship with the Queen.

Such a privilege of access is yours when you reconnect with your source, your heavenly Father. And your friendship is with One who is much greater than the Queen. It is with the Ultimate King, Jesus the Christ, the sovereign ruler of the eternal Kingdom of God (see Daniel 7: 9 – 14).

He publicly declared His friendship with his followers to all of the creation in the following words:

"No longer do I call you servants, because the servant does not know what his lord is doing; but I have called you friends, because all that I have heard from My Father I have made known to you." [95]

What a privilege we have, to be invited into the inner circle of the Almighty God, not as a servant or slave but as a friend.

And He reinforces this principle of His friendship by these words, *"Greater love has no one than this: that one lay down his life for his friends. You are My friends if you do what I command you."*[96]

However, to remain within this circle of influence, favour and blessing is conditional upon one thing... Obedience to Christ's commands.

He said, *"If you keep My commandments, you will abide in My love; just as I have kept My Father's commandments, and abide in His love. These things I have spoken to you that My joy may be in you, and your joy may be made full. This is My commandment, that you love one another, just as I have loved you."*[97]

In essence, pure, unadulterated love for God and for your fellow human is the secret to long-lasting success and your friendship with the King of kings.

THE QUEST FOR DOMINION

God's original purpose for mankind was and still is for him to exercise dominion over the earth. God states clearly, *"Let Us make man in Our image, according to Our likeness; let them have dominion over the fish of the sea, over the birds of the air, and over the cattle, over all the earth and over every creeping thing that creeps on the earth."*[98]

His unwavering mandate for you is to be the physical expression of His nature and character here on earth. And that nature is one of dominion (which is defined as 'Control or the Exercise of Control or Influence or Sovereignty).

Sovereignty refers to the executive authority that a king exercises over his territory.

Mankind lost the ability to dominate his environment by yielding to temptation and declaring independence from God's instructions – leading to Sin.

However, Christ Jesus restored our ability to once again fulfil our original mandate. His word reveals the saints in eternity proclaiming, *"You are worthy to take the scroll, And to open its seals; for You were slain, and have redeemed us to God by Your blood out of every tribe and tongue and people and nation, and have made us kings and priests to our God; and we shall reign on the earth."*[99]

However, there is a constant enemy, which is able… If and only If you permit it… to strip you of your ability to exercise dominion. ….. And it is not Satan. It is sin.

Satan merely presents the opportunities to sin, but only you can determine the outcome!

This is why the following admonition from Paul the apostle is critical:

"Do not let sin reign in your mortal body, that you should obey it in its lusts. And do not present your members as instruments of unrighteousness to sin, but present yourselves to God as being alive from the dead, and your members as instruments of righteousness to God. For sin shall not have dominion over you, for you are not under law but under grace." [100]

As a Child of God and citizen of His Kingdom, God has placed within you His Spirit of grace who enables you to live above the cravings of sin.

Your responsibility is to cultivate His presence so strongly in your life that every new day for the rest of your life is a manifestation of your quest for, and exercise of your divine mandate – Personal Dominion!

And as you exercise dominion over your own self, internal mastery will overflow into excellence in your service to humanity and external success.

Love...The Proof of Citizenship

In the beginning... God spoke the following words with which most people who have read the Bible are familiar:

"Let us make man in our image, after our likeness: and let them have dominion over the fish of the sea, and over the fowl of the air, and over the cattle, and over all the earth, and over every creeping thing that creeps upon the earth.

So God created man in his own image, in the image of God created he him; male and female created he them"[101]

Jesus, the Christ came to restore humanity to the original 'image and likeness' or nature of God which was lost by Adam in the Garden of Eden through disobedience to God's instruction.

One of the fundamental elements of the nature of God is love. His relationship with us is borne out of love and His very nature of love determined that He would send His son to die on a cross in order to redeem us from the clutches of the kingdom of darkness into which Adam's rebellion had thrust all of humanity.

Then He sent His Holy Spirit into our lives to infuse our being with His nature of love as His Word tells us.

"...The love of God is shed abroad in our hearts by the Holy Ghost which is given unto us."[102]

But as many people will readily admit, true, uncontaminated

God-kind of love is a missing factor in their experience with many religious people, Christians included.

Yet God admonishes us through Apostle James:

"If anyone says, "I love God", and hates his brother, he is a liar; for he who does not love his brother whom he has seen does not have the power to love God whom he has not seen. And this commandment we have from Him, that he who loves God should love his brother also." [103]

The message is clear... Pure, unadulterated, non-hypocritical love towards your fellow human is the only proof that you are a citizen of the Kingdom of God. Anything less as far as God is concerned is unacceptable.

And such love is available and accessible only through intimacy with The Holy Spirit.

THE SAME POWER...WORKS IN YOU

Whenever you remember Jesus Christ's victory over death, it is also great to remember that the events at Calvary were the fulfilment of an eternal purpose. The scriptures reveal that Christ is God's Lamb who was slain before the foundation of the world.[104]

Just as Jesus the Christ was born, crucified and resurrected on Easter Sunday, you were born in this generation to fulfil God's eternal purpose. You are not on planet earth, at this point in time, by accident or happenstance. You are here by divine appointment to fulfil God's original mandate and divine assignment.

In addition, just as God equipped Christ Jesus to fulfil His assignment, He also equips you to fulfil yours. His word says, *"...He that raised up Christ from the dead shall also quicken your mortal bodies by his Spirit that dwells in you."*[105]

The same power, which raised Christ from the dead, now works in you and by the working of His power in and through you; the potential for magnificent victory is yours.

In order to accomplish your purpose, protect your focus in three key areas of your life:

1) Never let anyone steal your dreams or the vision that God has placed in your heart. Peter was well-meaning when he told Jesus that he would not die on the cross but Jesus rebuked him with the words *"get behind me Satan."*[106] Jesus would not allow even one of his closest friends to deflect Him from pursuing His God-given assignment.

Don't let anyone steal your dreams through ridicule, deception or even outright opposition. Even if it seems a long wait, remember that the fulfilment of the vision is tied to an appropriate time in God's agenda (Habakkuk 2: 3), a kairos season. So do not give up on the dream. Hold fast… It will come to pass.

2) Never let anyone steal your time – It is all you've got. Whoever steals your time, steals your life. We are admonished to *"walk circumspectly, not as fools, but as wise, redeeming the time, because the days are evil."*[107] Jesus spent every available moment in the pursuit and fulfilment of His purpose. He stated, *"My Father is continually working, and I continue to work."*[108]

You must place great value on your time and use it effectively in the pursuit of knowledge, wisdom, associations and activities that advance you towards the accomplishment of your divine assignment.

3) Never let anyone or anything steal your relationship with God's Holy Spirit. He is the only one who can lead you into the fullness of truth[109], which will set you free from every hindrance to your life.

Because the Spirit of God works in you, you receive grace and power to live a life of great success and be a worthy ambassador of the Kingdom of God on earth.

GENERATIONAL BLESSING

A study of the Bible reveals clearly that God's relationship with mankind is always generational and He loves to deal with humans who think generationally.

In cultivating His relationship with Abraham, God said, *"For I know him, that he will command his children and his household after him, and they shall keep the way of the LORD, to do justice and judgment; that the LORD may bring upon Abraham that which he has spoken of him."*[110]

God chose Abraham because he would make decisions not simply to satisfy his present desires. Abraham would be mindful of the impact of his choices and decisions on future generations, and he would teach his children to do the same. Indeed one of the Bible's most potent definitions is, *"A good man leaves an inheritance to his children's children."*[111]

Our Heavenly Father delights in blessing us abundantly and sent His Son to accomplish this mission…Jesus came to give us the exceedingly abundant life.

This life is not just for you to enjoy today; it is for you pass on to your children and your children's children, but what choices and decisions are you making today in order to improve the chances of the next generation partaking of your blessings?

Integrity and Character: Many people, down through the ages, have generated great wealth in their lifetimes but in ways that have tarnished their reputation and left their children with a tremendous burden and stigma of a cursed name. God's word admonishes, *"A good name is rather to be chosen than great riches, and loving favour rather than silver and gold."*[112]

Walking in righteousness and integrity before God and man is the fundamental way to ensure a good name. Resolve to pursue your God-ordained purpose in ways that honour Him and enrich the lives of others. As much as lies within your power, *"follow peace with all men, and holiness, without which no man shall see the Lord."*[113]

Model truth and wisdom: Teach your children the same godly values the Bible advocates, not merely through lip service but through personal example. Let them experience the value of a parent or guardian who is committed to the discovery, pursuit and fulfilment of divine purpose. Let them experience the value of a parent who would rather pursue godly wisdom than waste their lives watching daily television soap operas.

As you, make the right choices outlined above, God's word promises in Psalm 115: 14, *"The LORD shall increase you more and more, you and your children."*

TARES OR WHEAT?

We live in an age when it seems increasingly difficult to understand what it really means to be a Christian. Many ignoble and immoral attitudes persist in the lives of many so-called Christians and many church institutions willingly accommodate or even promote the most brazen of moral perversity in the name of 'being relevant' to the society.

The current state of the 'universal church' is captured by the following parable: '*The Kingdom of Heaven may be compared to a man who sowed good seed in his field; but while the men were sleeping, his enemy came and sowed tares also among the wheat, and went away. But when the herb sprang up and bore fruit, then the tares appeared also. And the slaves of the householder came and said to him, "Lord, did you not sow good seed in your field? How then does it have tares?"*

And he said to them, "An enemy has done this!" And the slaves said to him, "Do you wish us, then, to go and collect them up?" But he said, "No, lest while you collect up the tares, you may root up the wheat with them. Allow both to grow together until the harvest; and at the time of the harvest, I will say to the reapers, 'First collect up the tares and bind them in bundles to burn them up; but gather the wheat into my barn.'"[114]

Evidently, God is not confused about the identity of those who are His children and true citizens of His Kingdom. Therefore, we must also constantly undertake honest self-examination to identify whether we are living our lives as tares or wheat. True faith in Christ Jesus is identified by a conscious and abiding desire to walk in obedience to truth.

Such obedience demands a significant measure of self-discipline in moral and spiritual conduct. Jesus put it this way, "*If anyone wishes to come after Me, let him deny himself, and take up his cross daily and follow Me.*"[115]

God has consistent expectations of us that are not subject to the shifting tides of human opinion. He has expressed them in many ways such as:

"*These are the things that you shall do; Speak every man the truth to his neighbour; execute the judgment of truth and peace in your gates: And let none of you imagine evil in your hearts against his neighbour; and love no false oath: for all these are things that I hate, says the LORD.*"[116]

Notice that these expectations are actually quite beneficial for a healthy society and not just some religious obligation.

Living by biblical principles should, therefore, underpin your contributions to your local community or other arena of influence because your community deserves it, just as much as you desire to please God and enjoy a blessed ultimate destiny.

Choose this day your destination, the fire or the barn… Will you be tares or wheat?

THE ASSIGNMENT

"Now the word of the LORD came unto Jonah the son of Amittai, saying, "Arise, go to Nineveh, that great city, and cry against it; for their wickedness is come up before me." But Jonah rose up to flee unto Tarshish from the presence of the LORD, and went down to Joppa; and he found a ship going to Tarshish..."[117]

The passage above describes the reaction of many people to the assignment God has committed into their hands. They recognize that within them is a message, an ability or an idea that will touch their world with hope and love. The assignment may be to those being destroyed by emotional trauma, social injustice, health problems, marital challenges, educational deficiency, financial lack or any other form of human captivity.

The fulfillment of your assignment, of course, carries the same risk that the prophet Jonah had to deal with; the risk that the people he was sent to would reject his message and perhaps even turn on him to destroy him.

And so we do the same thing Jonah did... We choose to head in another direction and engage in other activities in order to escape from the assignment.

Subsequently, in the story of Jonah, we see that such a choice brings with it dangerous consequences for three sets of people:

- **The people to whom you are sent** – The Ninevites needed Jonah's message to avert their destruction – Similarly, there is someone waiting at the other end of your obedience to your assignment to transform their future from despair and death to success and hope.

- **Your present companions** – Jonah's innocent companions on the ship to Tarshish (see Jonah 1: 4 – 5) experienced fear and devastation because of Jonah's presence on their ship. Is it possible that some people around you are experiencing continued danger because you are avoiding your responsibility to fulfill your divine assignment?

- **You** – Jonah's disobedience eventually caused him to be thrown overboard (see Jonah 1: 15 & 17) and end up in captivity in the belly of a whale – Refusal to pursue and fulfill your assignment leads into captivity of different sorts such as lack of peace, financial lack, physical, emotional or spiritual bondage.

The clarion call is going out today… Discover, pursue and fulfil your assignment on earth.

You were designed for it, born for it and called into the Kingdom of God to accomplish it. The assignment is why you are here.

THE PRICE OF IGNORANCE

"My people are destroyed for lack of knowledge: because you have rejected knowledge, I will also reject you, that you shall be no priest to me: seeing you have forgotten the law of your God, I will also forget your children."[118]

Many Christian believers are experiencing humiliating defeat in the financial arena of their lives, undergoing destruction in their relationships with other people or experiencing major setbacks in the area of health, while many more are being traumatized emotionally, physically or spiritually in other dimensions of their human existence.

If truth be told, too many Christians, who claim a relationship with an omniscient, omnipotent God are living lives of quiet desperation.

Yet, in the passage above, The All-knowing God never placed responsibility for such destruction on the one person that many Christians blame for their problems. Unlike many Christians, God never blamed the devil.

Instead, God states categorically that for many Christians, destruction is the heavy price they and their children are paying for willful ignorance and rejecting knowledge; and what a costly price to pay.

Question: So what is to be done to break the curse and penalty of ignorance?

Answer: Seek godly wisdom in the arena of life where you are experiencing destruction.

If you are hurting financially, seek out financial geniuses that have applied godly principles to achieve wealth and learn from them how to break free from financial bondage.

For those lacking in physical well-being, it is time to give those regular fast food outlets, pork chops and fried dumplings a miss and seek out a Health professional who is a time-tested epitome of well-being and learn the principles of good health from him or her.

As God continually reminds us, *"Wisdom is the principal thing; therefore get wisdom: and with all thy getting get understanding."*[119]

There are no excuses for destruction in the life of a believer because God invites, *"If any of you lacks wisdom, let him ask of God, Who gives to all men sincerely and without reproaching, and it will be given to him."*[120]

God has made His wisdom available to us. It may be hidden in a book, CD, DVD or person whom we must diligently learn from, but we must be humble enough to acknowledge our need and pursue knowledge in the right sources because the price of ignorance is too high.

Maximised Living

One thing that is certain about the LORD is that He absolutely loathes unproductive existence!

Most Christians are familiar with the story of the worthless servant and his talents (see Matthew 25: 14 – 29). But too many believers miss a central principle that the parable teaches us.

In the parable, the servant's master said, *"You wicked, lazy servant! So you knew that I harvest where I have not sown and gather where I have not scattered seed? Well then, you should have put my money on deposit with the bankers, so that when I returned, I would have received it back with interest."*[121]

This implies that there is a minimum acceptable level of productivity, which the master expected of his servants. This level was symbolised by a specific rate of interest achievable with the bankers.

And that is where most believers stop… at the minimum acceptable level of achievement.

But notice that the following words of praise and reward were reserved for those servants who maximised their productivity, *"Well done, good and faithful servant! You have been faithful with a few things; I will put you in charge of many things. Come and share your master's happiness!"*[122]

However, maximum productivity does not just happen. There are some fundamental requirements that simply must be satisfied in order for it to happen. One of these key requirements is a clearly stated and written goal.

God desired a nation that would achieve excellence in moral and spiritual conduct and wrote down His goals very clearly... we call them the Ten Commandments.

If God specified and documented His vision and goals for Israel, His chosen people, surely there must be some merit in you doing the same, if you hope to achieve significant success in your God-given purpose.

A study reportedly conducted by one of America's foremost universities showed that amongst the members of one of their graduating classes, 3% had written goals while 97% did not. Ten years later, the 3% had achieved greater success (in virtually all measurable dimensions of their lives) than the 97% combined.

Those 3% are not any more special than you or the other 97% in their graduating class. They simply applied a God-inspired, time-tested principle of setting productivity goals and then working towards them.

Jesus, the Christ demands that we be the best that we can be for His Kingdom. Spend time with the Holy Spirit in setting and pursuing your goals and experience a new dimension of focussed, maximised living.

THIRSTING FOR HIS PRESENCE

Jesus the Christ, our ultimate leader, outlined some of the principles required for every human to live effectively on earth as citizens of His Kingdom. Those principles have come to be known as the Beatitudes or 'the attitudes to be'.

One of those key principles is this: *"Blessed are they which do hunger and thirst after righteousness: for they shall be filled."*[123]

This is a principle that places a responsibility on every human that too many have often tried to place on God.

Righteousness is a spiritual law of success and an attribute that positions you for God's favour and blessings. It is a disposition to always do what is right, in the context of your relationships with your creator, your fellow humans and the fulfilment of your assignment on the earth.

God has promised to fill you with His righteousness, but the responsibility to hunger and thirst for it is yours and yours alone.

The idea of hunger and thirst is a most powerful description of what it takes to partake of the fullness of God's presence.

Hunger and thirst represent a fundamental level of desire that is so strong that it is willing to do whatever is required to satisfy it. It will settle for no substitutes, only that which can meet its need.

Indeed, it is a level of ardent desire, which, if left unsatisfied, leads to only one inevitable outcome – Death.

Picture in your mind a man trudging through the desert, at the end of his tether, literally dying of thirst. What alternatives could you offer him that would be acceptable and beneficial to him? Would he be interested in entertainment or wealth? What about religious or political activities or positions of authority? Most unlikely!

He would be interested in only one thing at that point in his life… Water!

That is the kind of desire that attracts God. He said through his prophet, *"And you shall seek me, and find me, when you shall search for me with all your heart."*[124]

He responds to a desire that demonstrates clearly that nothing else but the manifest, abiding presence of the Holy Spirit in your life will satisfy you.

Do you thirst that much for Him?

ABBA!

It is often said that if you wish to destroy a building, you don't go after the windows, the fixtures or the fittings within the building because those are easily replaceable… No, you go after the foundation. When the foundation is destroyed, the building is condemned.

Satan and his emissaries on the earth understand this principle, which is why they are orchestrating an all-out attack against the foundation of the family… Men.

Every effort is being undertaken to destroy men and their God-ordained role in the family structure either through the corruption of sexuality, through perverted versions of feminism or media-driven psychological warfare. These are aimed at keeping men from that which they most need in their lives… the presence and wisdom of God, which will infuse them with the confidence and grace to be real men.

At a time when the moral fabric of our societies are being compromised, and the foundations of the family is suffering a systematic and sustained attack, it is essential to restate and reinforce in our hearts, God's original pattern for human society.

God chose Abraham as His channel of blessing to the world for a particular reason, recorded for us in the Bible; "…*Seeing that Abraham shall surely become a great and mighty nation, and all the nations of the earth shall be blessed in him. Because I know him, that he will command his children and his household after him, and they shall keep the way of the LORD, to do justice and judgment; that the LORD may bring upon Abraham that which he has spoken of him."*[125]

God chose Abraham as His vessel through whom Christ would ultimately come because he would live and teach his children to keep the way of The LORD. That is the primary responsibility of every father.

Making money to feed and clothe your children, giving them an education, buying your family gifts and taking them on holidays is nice… but all these are nothing, compared to the responsibility of bringing your children up in the wisdom and righteousness of God.

You cannot abdicate this responsibility to the state educational system, the Sunday school teacher, your local pastor or the mother of the child… Fulfilling this tremendous spiritual responsibility is yours, and it is the gateway to the fulfilment of God's promises for your life.

May The Lord, who himself is the ultimate Father, who *'has sent forth the Spirit of his Son into your hearts, crying, Abba, Father'* fill you with His wisdom, grace and love and may you live as a worthy example of truth and righteousness to the next generation so that they can also lovingly call you … Dad, Abba!

Father…along with all within your sphere of influence, I salute you as you commit to fulfilling your awesome fatherhood mandate.

THE EVERLASTING KING

Daily news reports, analysis of political or economic events and the almost futile efforts of the leaders of many nations trying their hardest to keep the lid on the chaos within their respective nations, indicate clearly that we need leadership that transcends the ordinary.

Many nations are ravaged by AIDS, economic turbulence, moral decay, civil disobedience or some other form of internal malaise, which their leaders seem powerless to resolve.

At such a time as this, it is important to remember that there is a source of hope and wisdom that is available to every human.

God's word, the Bible foretold this ancient hope in the following words:

"For unto us a child is born, unto us a son is given: and the government shall be upon his shoulder: and his name shall be called Wonderful, Counsellor, The mighty God, The everlasting Father, The Prince of Peace. Of the increase of his government and peace there shall be no end, upon the throne of David, and upon his Kingdom, to order it, and to establish it with judgment and with justice from henceforth, even forever; The zeal of the LORD of hosts will perform this." [126]

This ancient hope is fulfilled in Jesus the Christ. As the prophet, Isaiah states, only the government (rulership, leadership) of Christ in the human heart and in a nation can bring real peace and justice.

Human leaders may try all they can to bring peace to their nation through the passing of laws or through military might, but there is no amount of legislation that can change the human heart defiled by sin. Only Jesus can do that.

Do not be dismayed by bad reports but be energised by your understanding that God has placed you on earth for such a time as this. You are in the world, but not limited by this world (John 17: 16) and you are the conduit through which the Everlasting King will extend His rule into your family, workplace, your neighbourhood and your nation.

You are the ambassador of the King, which confers upon you the responsibility to promote His interests exclusively wherever we are. Let the righteous King reign through you in your business success, educational attainments, political influence, family harmony or any other arena of human endeavour in which you function.

It is Time ...

As events in the world unfold, the sense of uncertainty and fear is increasing in the hearts of many. The world waits with bated breath to see what will happen between Iran and the United States as the leaders of Iran defy the world's demands to cease its drive to acquire nuclear technology.

Our governments stagger from one crisis to another in ways that makes one wonder about the quality of leadership that governs our nations. Daily news broadcasts reveal widespread religious or political conflict in many areas of the world, from Sudan to Sri Lanka, from Nepal to Nigeria many are waking to find themselves under siege.

Economic turbulence is escalating as oil prices fluctuate rapidly and nations like Greece, Hungary, Portugal, the United Kingdom and even the United States are bedevilled by massive national debt that threatens the financial futures of companies, nations and billions of people.

At times like this, it is critical to remember the following words of the Lord, "*These things I have spoken unto you, that in me you might have peace. In the world you shall have tribulation: but be of good cheer; I have overcome the world.*"[127]

You can walk in total peace because you are unique. You are in the world, but not of this world (John 17: 16). Your citizenship, and therefore your protection and provision is from heaven (Philippians 3: 20). You have been placed on earth at such a time as this for one purpose… to be an effective Ambassador of the Kingdom of God.

Now, more than ever, is the time for you to discover your assignment and walk in it.

It is time to shake off the lethargy induced by misdirected religious activity. It is time to wake up to your Kingdom responsibility. It is time to impact your home, neighbourhood and nation with the manifestation of your divine calling. It is time to reach your world with the love and power of The Holy Spirit.

It is Time!

Our world needs a message and a people of spiritual dynamism who do not walk in the same fear that other people in the world do.

Our world needs people who are dedicated to pursuing godly wisdom that transcends limited human understanding, and excellence in service to mankind in their chosen sphere of influence.

Our world needs You!

It is time for You to arise and become all that you were meant to Be.

OTHER BOOKS BY YEMI AKINSIWAJU

SCORECARD: ACHIEVING SUCCESS AND BALANCE IN A TURBULENT WORLD.

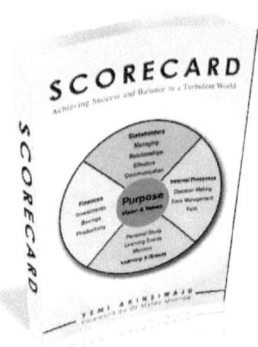

"This has to be one of the best and inspiring books that I have read in the last 2-3 years. I have a new spark for life and a greater zeal to succeed in all that I do. I will give the book to people I meet who express a genuine desire to move from being good to great and are willing to be stretched in all areas of their lives to achieve their goals."

Michael Smith MBE

(Award-winning Metropolitan Police Officer and Founder of Word for Weapons, UK)

ISBN: 978-0-59571-354-7   Hardcover
ISBN: 978-0-59547-807-1   Paperback

Available from Amazon, Barnes and Noble and other good bookstores

THE LEADERSHIP JIGSAW

"This immensely thought-provoking work gets to the heart of one of the principle challenges of our generation – that of effective and competent leadership."

Dr Myles Munroe

(International Leadership Statesman and Consultant to Governments)

ISBN: 978-0-9934482-1-8   Hardcover
ISBN: 978-0-9934482-0-1   Paperback

Available from Amazon, Barnes and Noble and other good bookstores

WATCH OUT FOR NEW BOOK

Leadership Gems

Inspirational Insights for The Frontline Leader

Volume 1

About the Author

YEMI AKINSIWAJU, known as the Leadership Catalyst, is the founder and CEO of DaySpring Consulting UK, a leadership consultancy dedicated to enhancing the leadership capacity of individuals and organizations.

Yemi sits on the Board of Directors of the International Third World Leaders Association (ITWLA), an organisation devoted to training and developing leaders in over eighty nations. He is the author of the following highly acclaimed books:

The Leadership Jigsaw: Transforming Mystery to Mastery

Scorecard: Achieving Success and Balance in a Turbulent World

Yemi is a multi-gifted international speaker, consultant and author, focussed on the crucial issues of leadership, personal transformation, organisational effectiveness, social and spiritual development. He has addressed audiences from over 50 nations as a conference speaker, seminar facilitator, mentor, trainer, coach and in television and radio appearances.

To book Yemi to speak at your event, contact him via:

Email: Yemi@YemiAkinsiwaju.com

For more information, visit www.YemiAkinsiwaju.com

References

1. Proverbs 25: 28
2. Matthew 6: 33
3. Luke 18: 8
4. Jeremiah 29: 11 – 13
5. Ephesians 2: 12
6. 1 John 3:1
7. Romans 8: 38 – 39
8. Jeremiah 31:3
9. See 2 Kings 18: 1 – 19: 36
10. 2 Corinthians 4:17
11. Hebrews 12: 2
12. Proverbs 23:7
13. See John 10: 30
14. Matthew 6: 5 – 7
15. Proverbs 24: 16
16. Psalm 34: 19
17. 1 Corinthians 9:24
18. 1 Corinthians 9: 25 & 27
19. 2 Timothy 4:7
20. 2 Corinthians 5: 7
21. Romans 10:17
22. Genesis 1: 11 – 12
23. See Proverbs 18: 21
24. Matthew 13:31
25. See Genesis 3: 15
26. See Genesis 37: 5 & Acts 7: 25
27. Ecclesiastes 3: 1
28. See Matthew 16: 3
29. See Judges 7: 2 –7
30. See Acts 13:2
31. 1 Chronicles 12:32
32. Joshua 1: 9
33. Deuteronomy 31: 6
34. See 2 Chronicles 20: 17
35. See John 16: 13
36. See 2 Samuel 6: 11
37. Matthew 3: 17
38. Malachi 4: 2 – 3
39. Proverbs 4: 7
40. Proverbs 19: 21
41. James 4: 3
42. Psalm 35: 27
43. Psalm 84: 11
44. 1 Kings 18: 42 – 45
45. 2 Timothy 3: 2 – 4
46. Matthew 24: 13
47. See Matthew 24: 13
48. Matthew 25:31 – 34
49. Mark 10:13 – 15
50. Acts 13: 22
51. 1 Kings 15:4 – 5
52. Hebrews 12: 2 – 3
53. Proverbs 29: 18a
54. Genesis 15: 5 – 6
55. Zechariah 13: 9

[56] See Ephesians 2: 10
[57] James 1: 2 – 4
[58] Philippians 2: 5 – 11
[59] see 1 Corinthians 2: 16
[60] Isaiah 6: 1 – 9
[61] See Acts 11:26
[62] 1 Corinthians 15:45
[63] Matthew 6: 10
[64] See Matthew 9: 35 & 4:23 & Matthew 10: 7
[65] Matthew 25: 31 - 34
[66] Matthew 7: 21
[67] Isaiah 46: 9 – 11
[68] Isaiah 55: 10 – 12
[69] Psalm 139: 16 – 17
[70] Ephesians 2: 10
[71] Luke 13: 2 – 5
[72] Hebrews 1: 1 – 2
[73] Daniel 11: 32
[74] John 14: 15 – 17
[75] 2 Timothy 3: 1 – 5
[76] See Matthew 5: 14
[77] Romans 14: 17
[78] Psalm 146: 1 – 10
[79] Exodus 15: 17 – 18
[80] Deuteronomy 8: 3
[81] See Matthew 25: 14 – 30
[82] Matthew 25: 19
[83] Matthew 25: 21
[84] Matthew 5: 8
[85] Matthew 5: 23 – 24
[86] 1 Peter 5: 5
[87] Proverbs 4: 23
[88] Matthew 6: 33
[89] Exodus 4: 2 – 4
[90] Exodus 4: 20
[91] Psalm 14: 1a
[92] Psalm 111: 10
[93] John 16: 33
[94] See Romans 14:17
[95] John 15: 15
[96] John 15: 13 – 14
[97] John 15: 10 – 12
[98] Genesis 1: 26
[99] Revelation 5: 9
[100] Romans 6: 12 – 14
[101] Genesis 1: 26 – 27
[102] Romans 5: 5
[103] 1 John 4: 20 – 21
[104] See Revelation 13:8
[105] Romans 8: 11
[106] See Mark 8: 33
[107] Ephesians 5: 15 – 16
[108] John 5: 17
[109] See John 8: 32 & 16: 13
[110] Genesis 18: 19
[111] Proverbs 13: 22
[112] Proverbs 22: 1
[113] Hebrews 12: 14
[114] Matthew 13: 24 – 30
[115] Luke 9: 23
[116] Zechariah 8: 16 – 17
[117] Jonah 1: 1 – 3
[118] Hosea 4: 6
[119] Proverbs 4: 7
[120] James 1: 6
[121] Matthew 25: 26 – 27
[122] Matthew 25: 21 & 23
[123] Matthew 5: 6
[124] Jeremiah 29: 13
[125] Genesis 18: 18 – 19
[126] Isaiah 9: 6 – 8
[127] John 16: 33